WITHDRAWN FROM STOCK
Libraries for Users

CHANDOS
INFORMATION PROFESSIONAL SERIES

Series Editor: Ruth Rikowski
(email: Rikowskigr@aol.com)

Chandos' new series of books are aimed at the busy information professional. They have been specially commissioned to provide the reader with an authoritative view of current thinking. They are designed to provide easy-to-read and (most importantly) practical coverage of topics that are of interest to librarians and other information professionals. If you would like a full listing of current and forthcoming titles, please visit our web site www.chandospublishing.com or email info@chandospublishing.com or telephone +44 (0) 1223 499140.

New authors: we are always pleased to receive ideas for new titles; if you would like to write a book for Chandos, please contact Dr Glyn Jones on email gjones@chandospublishing.com or telephone number +44 (0) 1993 848726.

Bulk orders: some organisations buy a number of copies of our books. If you are interested in doing this, we would be pleased to discuss a discount. Please email info@chandospublishing.com or telephone +44 (0) 1223 499140.

Libraries for Users

Services in academic libraries

LUISA ALVITE AND
LETICIA BARRIONUEVO

CP

CHANDOS
PUBLISHING

Oxford Cambridge New Delhi

Chandos Publishing
Hexagon House
Avenue 4
Station Lane
Witney
Oxford OX28 4BN
UK
Tel: +44 (0) 1993 848726
Email: info@chandospublishing.com
www.chandospublishing.com

Chandos Publishing is an imprint of Woodhead Publishing Limited

Woodhead Publishing Limited
80 High Street
Sawston
Cambridge CB22 3HJ
UK
Tel: +44 (0) 1223 499140
Fax: +44 (0) 1223 832819
www.woodheadpublishing.com

First published in 2011

ISBN:
978 1 84334 595 4

British Library Cataloguing-in-Publication Data.
A catalogue record for this book is available from the British Library.

Typeset by RefineCatch Limited, Bungay, Suffolk
Printed in the UK and USA.

Printed in the UK by 4edge Limited - www.4edge.co.uk

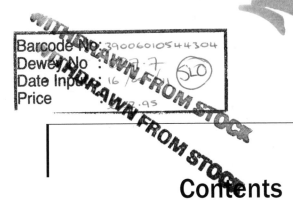
Contents

List of figures

Preface

The intention of this publication is to present the current status of services provided by university libraries. We have striven to explore the way in which academic libraries are adapting their traditional services and adding new ones in order to adapt to the demands of the new model of society, the Knowledge Society, and the new environment in higher education marked by globalisation and competitiveness.

The first few chapters shed light on academic institutions and describe the unstoppable trend towards reinforcing higher education's commitment to assessment and quality in the quest for excellence in teaching and research. As a key part of the institution, the university library is one of the prime indicators for measuring the quality of the institution. Its assessment is, in turn, linked to user satisfaction and therefore directly related to the quality of the services provided.

Users and their needs are the engines of change in the library's role and in academic information services. The challenge of the new teaching-learning paradigm espoused by the European Higher Education Area and the challenges posed by e-science are asking that library services not only support but also truly foster learning and research. The very concept of academic library, already thrown into upheaval by the digital revolution, is taking on a new guise as the learning and research resource centre, designed so that end users receive the highest quality service.

We have grouped three crucial services under the heading of The Challenge of Enhancing Traditional Services: catalogues, reference services and marketing. The changes in the access and information retrieval today, dominated by intuitive interfaces and powerful search engines, pose a major challenge for OPACs, a challenge that requires us to adjust the design of the system to users' real behaviour, study their interoperability with the library's other electronic collections and reflect on their possible inclusion in web-based engines and projects immersed in the semantic web.

In turn, the information desk and reference collection have joined the developments in virtual reference services, which use tools like instant messaging, chats and specific programmes wholly designed for this purpose to ensure the efficacy and user-friendliness of the service. There is no question that innovative, creative initiatives must become allied through the use of marketing techniques and strategies in order to make the library service more effective and boost its clientele. We can witness an increasingly positive attitude and greater involvement among professionals in performing the jobs related to promotion and dissemination of the services provided.

The last chapter addresses services that we regard as essential within today's academic library. This includes strategies like institutional repositories, which contribute to the institution's visibility and public value by promoting the dissemination of the results of its activities and contributing to the reform of the scientific communication system; and in-house digital collections, which foster access to the institution's collections, often of incalculable historical value, with the library helping to disseminate and preserve them.

Equally important is the role that the library should play to ensure that users acquire competences and skills related to the access, use and evaluation of information. Information Literacy is now a service that goes beyond traditional patron training, a new challenge for librarians and for the library as a learning centre. Finally, the inclusion of social technologies and Web 2.0 services provides us with a unique chance to reach a wider audience, get users to participate as creators of contents and develop services with an added value.

Despite any oversights and shortcomings, we hope that this publication will be useful for readers interested in reflecting on the role of university libraries and the challenges, strategies and future perspectives that serve to reinforce the services provided for users, and in maintaining the library's leadership in the provision of information.

About the authors

Luisa Alvite, PhD, is an assistant professor in the Department of Library and Information Science at the University of León, Spain. She has focused her research interests on Information Retrieval, Interfaces, Electronic Libraries and Digital Contents. She has published several works related to these subjects in different congress proceedings and scientific journals.

Leticia Barrionuevo has a degree in Information Science from the University Carlos III of Madrid. She completed a doctorate on 'Knowledge Management and Transfer in the Organizations' and she is now writing her doctoral dissertation on evaluation of institutional repositories. She has been in charge of the Library of the Faculty of Philosophy and Letters in the University of León from 2005, and she has worked in the field of archives and libraries for more than nine years. She is involved in the design and implementation of the open and institutional digital archive and she lectures on electronic resources and Open Access initiatives to university teaching staff.

The authors may be contacted at:

E-mail: *luisa.alvite@unileon.es*
        buffl@unileon.es

Academic library services: quality and leadership

Universities in a globalised setting

Even though there is no agreement on the elements that comprise excellence in higher education, in the past decade we have witnessed a veritable explosion in university rankings. We can cite, for example, the Academic Ranking of World Universities (ARWU)[1] published by the Center for World-Class Universities and the Institute of Higher Education of Shanghai Jiao Tong University. This system emphasises publications, citations and academic prizes, especially in science and technology. The QS World University Rankings[2] relies heavily on academic peer review (which accounts for 40 per cent). The SCImago Institutions Rankings (SIR)[3] is built with data from Elsevier database Scopus. The SIR 2009 World Report ranks the best 2,000 worldwide research institutions and organisations and analyses their research performance in the period 2003–7 through five global output indicators. In turn, Webometrics Ranking of World Universities[4] produced by the Cybermetrics Lab (National Research Council of Spain), offers information about more than 8,000 universities according to their web presence, a computerised assessment of the scholarly contents and visibility and impact of the whole university web domain.

Obviously, the results are not all similar because of the relative weight assigned to the indicators used, which means that we can find a single institution with widely divergent rankings depending on the list chosen. A careful statistical analysis of international ranking concludes that there is broad consensus about the first 10–12 universities, but after that the lists begin to diverge. The lack of an absolute set of performance criteria may mean that 'world class' standing will probably be based more on academic reputation than on a set of formal standards (Mohrman et al., 2008).

The popularity of this kind of ranking is a clear sign of the globalisation of knowledge and the internationalisation of university teaching. The more traditional comparisons among institutions within a single country have been eclipsed by observations that scrutinise a university's position beyond the restricted political or linguistic frontiers.

In this context, networks of excellence have arisen. The International Alliance of Research Universities (IARU)[5] is perhaps the network that best illustrates this phenomenon. It was set up in 2006 and includes ten leading research universities: Australian National University, ETH Zurich, National University of Singapore, Peking University, University of California at Berkeley, University of Cambridge, University of Copenhagen, Oxford University, University of Tokyo and Yale University. Equally noteworthy is the fact that several universities have set up a group that they define as the 'Emerging Global Model (EGM)' for the university of the twenty-first century. Mohrman et al. (2008) argue that the development of the EGM is both a response to and an influence upon the major factors in contemporary society. EGM universities look worldwide for research partners, graduate students, prospective faculty and financial resources. This group of global universities will form an elite subset in a larger universe of higher education institutions. The growth of international university associations demonstrates the interdependence of EGM universities through transnational activities.

Without downplaying the controversy over the methodology used in this kind of ranking, we believe that they are yet another element reinforcing higher education's commitment to evaluation and quality and acting as an incentive and stimulus in the quest for excellence in institutions' teaching and research. In European universities, the political measures aimed at intensifying research competitiveness and restructuring higher education systems have been ratcheted up in recent years. A well-known multinational organisation is the European Union's Erasmus Mundus Programme,[6] a cooperation and mobility initiative that enhances the quality of European higher education and promotes the European Union as a centre of excellence in learning around the world.

The EFQM Model of Excellence was established as a guide for rating the organisations that vied for the European Quality Award created by the European Foundation for Quality Management (EFQM).[7] On 29 September 2009, the results of the revision of the EFQM Excellence Model were presented and a new version of the 2010 EFQM Model was previewed at the Annual EFQM Forum in Brussels. This model will coexist with the current model dating from 2003 throughout 2010.

Today EFQM is being accepted as a management model by organisations that are seeking institutional excellence, and it is a benchmark in Europe for excellence as its design encompasses the most up-to-date management practices within an organisation. This model is based on self-assessment and defines the parameters that must be taken into account in order to assess the maturity of the management system within any organisation.

EFQM applies the concept of quality to higher education by defining quality as the degree to which a continuum of differentiating features inherent in higher education fulfils a given need or expectation. Quality is an asset of an institution or programme that fulfils the standards preset by an accreditation agency. In order to be properly measured, this usually involves the evaluation of teaching, learning, management and results.[8]

The European Association for Quality Assurance in Higher Education (ENQA)[9] was established in 2000 to promote European cooperation in the field of quality assurance. The idea for the association originates from the European Pilot Project for Evaluating Quality in Higher Education (1994–5), which demonstrated the value of sharing and developing experiences in the area of quality assurance. Subsequently, the idea was given momentum by the Recommendation of the Council (98/561/EC of 24 September 1998) on European cooperation in quality assurance in higher education and by the Bologna Declaration of 1999. The European Commission has, through grant support, financed the activities of ENQA since the very beginning. The third edition of Standards and Guidelines for Quality Assurance in the European Higher Education Area was published in 2009 (European Association for Quality Assurance in Higher Education – ENQA, 2009).

Likewise, the European Quality Assurance Register for Higher Education (EQAR)[10] aims at increasing the transparency of quality assurance and thus enhancing trust and confidence in European higher education. EQAR will list quality assurance agencies that operate in Europe and have proven their credibility and reliability in a review against the European Standards and Guidelines for Quality Assurance (ESG). It publishes and manages a register of quality assurance agencies that substantially comply with the European Standards and Guidelines for Quality Assurance (ESG) to provide the public with clear and reliable information on quality assurance agencies operating in Europe.

The different European Union member states have their own national and/or regional quality evaluation and accreditation agencies with the goal of contributing to improving the quality of the higher education systems through the evaluation, certification and accreditation of their programmes, faculty, institutions and services, including libraries.[11]

In a competitive and internationalised context, evaluation processes can spring from a regulatory requirement – either regional or nationwide – or can be conducted on the initiative of the institution itself in an effort to consolidate or accentuate the university's prestige. The library must have solid grounding in quality management in order to adapt to the demands of the evaluations it might be subjected to in order to support the institutional strategies.

Quality in academic libraries

A university library is a key element in the institution it serves and is one of the indisputable indicators for measuring its quality. For this reason, as a provider of services that make teaching activities, learning and research activities possible, and with responsibilities in providing lifelong training for graduates, the library is fully immersed in the processes of quality assessment in higher education.

The most frequently cited definition of quality is the one contained in the ISO 9000 standard (ISO 9000, 2005), in which quality is described as 'the consistent conformance of a product or service to a given set of standards or expectations'. In turn, the ISO 11620:1998 (ISO 11620, 1998) norm views quality as the set of all the characteristics of a product or service that affect the library's capacity to meet either stated or implicit needs.

The principles and practice of quality management have evolved in recent decades. As Gimeno Perelló (2009: 40–1) points out, four significant stages in quality management can be pinpointed: inspection, quality control, quality assurance and finally total quality management (TQM) and management of organisational excellence. University libraries in the United States were the first ones to introduce quality models, systems and plans into their management. At first, library quality was viewed as the quality of the technical processes and, to a lesser extent, the services. This conception has gradually evolved towards quality in patron satisfaction, as, indeed, a twenty-first century academic library must be a highly efficient organisation oriented towards its patrons.

However, the perception of a library's quality will differ among stakeholder groups, as underscored by Poll and Boekhorst (2007: 15):

> Users see library quality according to their experience with the service they use. They will not care for the efficiency of background processes, but for the effective delivery of services. The funding or parent institution will be interested in the library's benefit to the institution and in the library's cost-effectiveness. Staff, on the other hand, will rate the libraries' quality by their working conditions, by adequate offers for further education, and by an efficient organisation.

Along these lines, the ACRL Standards for Libraries in Higher Education (2004) states that a comprehensive assessment requires the involvement of all categories of library users as well as a sampling of non-users. The choice of clientele to be surveyed and questions to be asked should be made by the library administration and staff with the assistance of an appropriate advisory committee. Questions should relate to how well the library supports its mission and how well it achieves its goals and objectives.

Methods of evaluating quality

Evaluation requires the use of a standard, rigorous methodology that systematically yields objective information, both qualitative and quantitative, which makes decision-making possible. It is wise for the library to have an evaluation and improvement plan.

The evaluation methodology is not an end in itself; rather it is a way of helping to achieve and ensuring sound end results. A quality evaluation plan with an ad hoc methodology cannot be called a plan per se; rather, it is an effort that is lacking a tool or procedure to guide it (Gimeno Perelló, 2009: 79).

ISO 9000 quality norms

Since 1987, the year when they appeared, these norms have become increasingly widely used, especially in business, which has meant that a rising number of information services that support companies are also managed according to these norms. They are a set of rules mainly targeted at comprehensive quality management systems or TQM. They began to be used in libraries in the United Kingdom and the Nordic countries in the late 1980s.

According to Balagué Mola (2007), the ISO 9000 series encompasses a variety of norms, but today the only certifiable one is the ISO 9001:2000 (the fourth version is the ISO 9001:2008). ISO 9001 is being adopted by public institutions; it is based on process management and it is applied in the libraries of higher education institutions of all sizes, regardless of whether the library system is made up of a single library or an extensive network with numerous service points and locations scattered about several campuses. The conclusions of the exhaustive study by Balagué Mola which surveys quality management based on the ISO 9001 norm in libraries of higher education institutions in up to 34 countries stresses that the factors holding the greatest weight when deciding to launch a certification process are the desires to improve the quality of the library services and to improve the university's strategy on quality matters. External factors like the existence of other libraries with this certification and the prestige of the norm are not so decisive and are secondary when deciding on certification. Instead, what prevail are factors aimed at improving the organisation internally. In short, the libraries earn the certification in order to have a true, comprehensive system of quality management, not only a marketing tool.

According to Balagué, the implementation of ISO 9001 is a major first step in implementing other more holistic quality initiatives which libraries must be willing to consider. The future of ISO 9001 in libraries does not involve a restrictive position, rather an integrative one within the framework of TQM that is open to other techniques and models.

EFQM Model

As mentioned above, this was designed by the European Foundation for Quality Management. It is one of the most widely used evaluation methodologies in Europe. The model is based on self-assessment, and its goal is to help organisations get to know themselves better and as a result to improve their performance. The EFQM Guide outlines three phases or stages of evaluation: self-evaluation or internal evaluation (which comes with tables of figures and indicators to be used and the excellence matrix), external evaluation (which includes tools prepared to facilitate the committee's efforts at analysis and synthesis) and the Final Evaluation Report (which asks for an assessment of the contrast between the library's internal and external evaluation processes; it also includes a section to synthesise the results on each sub-criterion, and another for strong and weak points; it finally includes an improvement plan).

The strongest points of this model according to Gimeno Perelló (2009: 95–96) are the following:

- It shows the status of the library on its pathway towards excellence, helping to identify both problems and their solutions.
- It serves as a foundation for the planning and management process as it enables strong and weak points to be detected and actions to be prepared to improve them, as well as the possibility of benchmarking.
- The model is transversal in nature.
- It provides management of external alliances, especially in contexts in which networks, consortia and other forms of partnership are particularly important.

In short, TQM as a new management philosophy encompasses all the library's activities, processes and services in an effort towards constant improvement. It goes beyond the organisation itself to also include suppliers and clients, a concept that includes both the person who receives the product and anyone who takes part in the productive process. The four basic points of TQM are: keeping the improvement of products and services as the main objective; acting so that quality does not depend on inspections; constantly training staff; and eliminating barriers among services. This situation requires the library to constantly strive to adapt and work with its users through innovation, creativity and cooperation (Pinto et al., 2007).

User-oriented quality

As Brophy (2005: 60–2) stresses, it is fundamental for quality management that 'quality' be understood as being inextricably linked to user satisfaction; the user is the focus of judgements about quality. Additionally, higher and further education institutions are working in the public sector, where much of their responsibility is to society as a whole. For this reason, Brophy broadly interprets the academic library's stakeholders by including, for example, former students, the higher education funding councils, the national and international research community, the local or regional library community, etc.

User satisfaction is measured by the sound quality of the services, including: customer care, bibliographic reference, virtual reference, user training, information literacy, reading room, loans, conditions of facilities, OPAC, website, digital collections, accessibility, etc. Yet academic libraries' quality plans must also respond to crucial issues like: the degree to which the library is integrated into teaching in the case of Europe with the European Higher Education Area (EHEA), the degree to which it is integrated into research, its degree of commitment with the institution, the collection's fit with the curricula of the degrees offered, open access repository and quantity and quality of accessible materials, ease of electronic publishing of research studies and publications, the library's integration into the classroom or virtual campus.

Quality in the library means having the state-of-the-art evaluation mechanisms and tools that enable libraries to act on the results. Furthermore, quality must be particularly linked to knowing and understanding users' needs and expectations. The library must have an organisation, processes and systems that are properly structured and targeted at user satisfaction.

Library staff involvement and a proactive attitude are necessary for working with a new philosophy with quality, evaluation and strategic planning as the cornerstones. As part of the policy of total quality, improvement groups can be set up in libraries as a tool for improving their efficiency, optimising their resources and establishing methodologies and instruments for learning more about users' needs, specifications and requirements. Improvement groups foster teamwork and especially participation and consensus. University libraries have also sought a greater commitment to users by drawing up and publicising menus of services that include a list of services available as well as specific quality pledges, along with the indicators that are used to measure their degree of fulfilment.

For years, university libraries have been gathering statistics that have gradually become more comprehensive and reliable. These instruments are extremely important and today comprise key databases in decision-making within the sector. The ARL statistics have been collected and published for the members of the Association every year since 1961–2.[12] The Society of College, National and University Libraries (SCONUL) in the United Kingdom began to gather statistics in 1987. Creaser (2009) lists a wide range of uses for the SCONUL statistical products, which are divided into three groups: service evaluation used by individual libraries, benchmarking and advocacy.

As Poll and Boekhorst (2007: 31–42) accurately point out, libraries have always been capable of calculating the input into their services (funding, staff, collections, space, equipment) and the output of those services (loans, visits, downloads, reference transactions, etc.). Measures have also been developed for assessing the quality of library services and the cost-efficiency of the library's performance. Performance measurement evaluates whether a library is effective and efficient in delivering its services. However, they also caution that the quantity of use and quality of performance do not yet prove that users benefited from their interaction with a library. Measuring impact or outcome means as reflected in Figure 1.1, going a step further and trying to assess the effect of services on users and on society. Outcome or impact means that there is a change in user's skills, knowledge or behaviour.

Poll and Boekhorst speak about short-term effects (find relevant information, solve a problem, save time in their work, gain searching skills, gain self-reliance in using information, etc.) and long-term effects of using library services (higher information literacy, higher academic or professional success, changes in attitudes and motivation, and changes in information behaviour). The changes can be represented in a pyramidal fashion, ranging from the cognitive impact (knowledge acquisition) to changes in attitudes and opinions, and finally to changes in behaviour.

Determining whether a library provides good service has been a constant concern for several decades now. In Europe, the point of departure was the Follett Report (Joint Funding Council, 1993), which stressed the need for a strategic change in British libraries and recommended the use of a series of coherent, generic performance indicators. Since then, major studies like the International Federation of Library Associations and Institutions (IFLA) and ISO have

Figure 1.1   Measuring impact or outcome

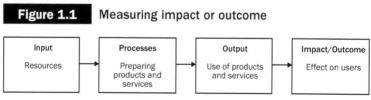

Source: Poll and Boekhorst (2007: 31).

been joined by numerous projects and proposals, including EQUINOX,[13] eVALUEd,[14] COUNTER,[15] etc. (Poll and Payne, 2006; Poll and Boekhorst, 2007).

Regardless of whether the methods are quantitative or qualitative, we agree with Brophy (2005: 194) on the imperative need to pay special attention to how the indicators are interpreted. Evaluating the performance of a university library is a matter of enormous complexity that goes beyond individual qualities and that after years of experience seems to be headed towards a synthesis in which the best of the different methodological approaches are being used.

Because of its prominence and international expansion, the Model LibQual+®[16] deserves a special mention of its own. It dates back to 1999 as a project to adapt the ServQual model developed by Texas A&M University (TAMU) and Association of Research Libraries (ARL). It is a standard for measuring users' degree of satisfaction with the services offered by libraries. It is a suite of services that libraries use to solicit, track, understand and act upon users' opinions of service quality. These services are offered to the library community by the ARL. The programme's centrepiece is a rigorously tested web-based survey bundled with training that helps libraries assess and improve library services, change organisational culture and market the library. The 22 core survey items measure user perceptions of service quality in three dimensions: Service Affect, Information Control and Library as Place. To ensure the validity of the responses, each dimension is assessed through a variety of questions. The goals of LibQUAL+® are:

- to foster a culture of excellence in providing library service;
- to help libraries better understand perceptions of library service quality;
- to collect and interpret library user feedback systematically over time;

- to provide libraries with comparable assessment information from peer institutions;
- to identify best practices in library service; and
- to enhance library staff members' analytical skills for interpreting and acting on data.

More than 1,000 libraries have participated in LibQUAL+®, and the model has been implemented in 17 countries. Kyrillidou et al. (2008) conducted an exhaustive survey of the articles published that document the use of this model. The most important development in LibQUAL+® in recent years took place in 2008 when the ARL/Texas A&M research and development team tested an alternative form of the conventional LibQUAL+® survey, called 'LibQUAL+® Lite' (Thompson et al., 2009). The Lite protocol uses item sampling methods to gather data on all 22 LibQUAL+® core items, while only requiring given individual users to respond to a subset of the 22 core questions. The LibQUAL+® Lite protocol is being implemented in such a manner that individual libraries will determine what percentage of their users will randomly be assigned the traditional LibQUAL+® protocol and what percentage will randomly be assigned the LibQUAL+® Lite protocol.

Leading libraries in service provision

Quality is the users' perception when comparing a product or service with others and with their own expectations. Therefore, it is a social construct. Quality is always relative, it is dynamic in nature and it is constantly evolving. Higher education and university libraries are consumer goods governed by market laws and the attitudes and preferences that influence citizens' perceptions. For this reason, a quality management system must make it possible for the services that a library provides to be constantly adapted and improved. We must evaluate in order to evolve along with our users.

The concept of leadership bears a close relationship to quality management, so the EFQM model is grounded on strong leadership exerted over policy planning and the strategy for managing human resources, material resources and partner organisations with the purpose of improving the processes. In the end, this will lead to improved customer satisfaction, providing key performance results for the organisation, which thus learns from itself and constantly improves on its pathway to excellence.

The challenges and demands of higher education institutions in a setting which is internationalised and competitive, as mentioned above, require libraries focused on users with rigorous quality policies that enable them to act as leading organisations within the university itself and in society as a whole. It should come as no surprise that Rowley and Roberts (2009: 197) believe that 'higher education and academic librarianship are being re-shaped by the actions of professionals and the institutions in which they work'. They add that 'the information profession and its members have no choice but to exercise influential leadership, to act in a more entrepreneurial style, seeking out ways in which to add value and make significant contributions to the organization's goals that go beyond the traditional parameters of an information service' (Rowley and Roberts, 2009: 198).

University libraries are facing complex challenges stemming primarily from the digital environment, which has drastically transformed the context of education, access to information resources and the way the library traditionally operated to support learning and research. We believe that this challenge must be seized upon as a chance to set up ambitious plans that reinforce library services creatively and innovatively.

Notes

1. *http://www.arwu.org/*
2. *http://www.topuniversities.com/university-rankings/*
3. *http://www.scimagoir.com/pdf/sir_2009_world_report.pdf*
4. *http://www.webometrics.info/*
5. *http://www.iaruni.org/*
6. *http://eacea.ec.europa.eu/erasmus_mundus/*
7. *http://www.efqm.org*
8. EFQM Excellence Model. Adaptation to Public Administration. *http://www.aeval.es/comun/pdf/Guia_EFQM_corta_04_06.pdf*
9. *http://www.enqa.eu/*
10. *http://www.eqar.eu/*
11. *http://www.enqa.eu/agencies.lasso*
12. *http://www.arl.org/stats/annualsurveys/arlstats/index.shtml*
13. *http://equinox.dcu.ie/*
14. *http://www.evalued.bcu.ac.uk/*
15. *http://www.projectcounter.org/*
16. *http://www.libqual.org/*

References

Association of College & Research Libraries (ACRL) (2004) *ACRL Standards for Libraries in Higher Education.* Available from: *http://www.ala.org/ala/mgrps/divs/acrl/standards/standardslibraries.cfm.*

Balagué Mola, N. (2007) 'El uso de la norma de calidad ISO 9001 en las bibliotecas de instituciones de educación superior', *BiD: Textos universitaris de biblioteconomia i documentació*, 19. Available from: *http://www2.ub.edu/bid/consulta_articulos.php?fichero=19balag2.htm.*

Brophy, P. (2005) *The Academic Library*, 2nd edn. London: Facet.

Creaser, C. (2009) 'UK higher education library statistics', in M. Heaney (ed.), *Library Statistics for the Twenty-First Century World*. Munchen: K.G. Saur, pp. 261–72.

European Association for Quality Assurance in Higher Education (ENQA) (2009) *Standards and Guidelines for Quality Assurance in the European Higher Education Area*, 3rd edn. Helsinki: ENQA. Available from: *http://www.enqa.eu/files/ESG_3edition%20(2).pdf*.

Gimeno Perelló, J. (2009) *Evaluación de la calidad en bibliotecas: compromiso con lo público*. Buenos Aires: Alfagrama.

International Organization for Standardization (1998) *ISO 1620:1998: Information and Documentation: Library Performance Indicators*. Genève: International Organization for Standardization.

International Organization for Standardization (2005) *ISO 9000:2005: Quality Management Systems, Fundamentals and Vocabulary*. Genève: International Organization for Standardization.

Kyrillidou, M., Cook, C. and Rao, S.S. (2008) 'Measuring the quality of library service through LibQUAL+®', in M.L. Radford and P. Snelson (eds), *Academic Library Research*. Chicago: Association of College and Research Libraries, pp. 253–301.

Joint Funding Council's Libraries Review Group (1993) *The Follett Report: A Report for Higher Education Founding Council for England, Scottish Higher Education Funding Council, Higher Education Funding Council for Wales, Department of Education for Northern Ireland*. Available from: *http://www.cpa.ed.ac.uk/reports/follett/*.

Mohrman, K., Ma, W. and Baker, D. (2008) 'The Research University in Transition: The Emerging Global Model', *Higher Education Policy*, 21(1): 5–27. Available from: *http://www.palgrave-journals.com/hep/journal/v21/n1/pdf/8300175a.pdf*.

Pinto, M., Balagué, N. and Anglada, L. (2007) 'Evaluación y calidad en las bibliotecas universitarias: experiencias españolas entre 1994–2006', *Revista Española de Documentación Científica*, 30(3): 364–83.

Poll, R. and Boekhorst, P. (2007) *Measuring Quality: Performance Measurement in Libraries*, 2nd rev. edn. Munchen: K.G. Saur.

Poll, R. and Payne, P. (2006) 'Impact measures for libraries and information services', *Library Hi Tech*, 24(4): 547–62.

Rowley, J. and Roberts, S. (2009) 'Influential leadership for academic libraries', in J.R. Griffiths and J. Crave (eds), *Access, Delivery, Performance: The Future of Libraries without Walls*. London: Facet, pp. 197–214.

Thompson, B., Kyrillidou, M. and Cook, C. (2009) 'Item sampling in service quality assessment surveys to improve response rates and reduce respondent burden: The "LibQUAL+® Lite example" ', *Performance Measurement & Metrics*, 10(1): 6–16. Available from: *http://libqual. org/documents/admin/pmm10-1_LQlite.pdf.*

2

Users: learning and researching in the digital age

The new teaching-learning model in European higher education

In recent years, the notion of the European Higher Education Area (EHEA) has become the conceptual framework of the new paradigm of higher education. It is simultaneously a challenge and an opportunity to change the university, and consequently the university library.

The construction of the EHEA began with the Sorbonne Joint Declaration[1] on 25 May 1998, which was later endorsed by the commitment of the Ministers of Education of the European Union (EU) member states in the Bologna Declaration[2] dated 19 June 1999. The ministers agreed to support policies in their respective countries to achieve the following goals:

- To adopt a degree system that was readily comprehensible and comparable in order to encourage employment and the competitiveness of the European higher education system.

- To establish a system based essentially on two main cycles: undergraduate and graduate.

- To adopt a shared credit system, called the European Credit Transfer System (ECTS), as the most suitable way of promoting further mobility among students.

- To promote mobility and the free exchange of students, faculty and administrative staff by adopting recognition mechanisms.

- To promote European cooperation as a guarantee of quality.

- To promote the European dimension in higher education, particularly targeted at curriculum development, inter-institutional cooperation and the integration of training and research.

These six objectives were joined by three more contained in the Prague Communiqué[3] dated 19 May 2001:

- Lifelong learning.

- The active role of universities, institutions and students in the convergence process.

- To promote the EHEA through quality systems and certification and accreditation mechanisms.

These principles were ratified at successive meetings held in Berlin[4] (2003), Bergen[5] (2005) and London[6] (2007), and they spurred a revision of the educational systems in the different EU member states. The last summit held was in April 2009 in Leuven/Louvain-la-Neuve.[7] This gathering reaffirmed the soundness of the Bologna Process and stressed that the Community institutions must make known the true benefits of this plan, one of whose main challenges is improving information.

This new model includes a series of key factors that distinguish it from the prevailing system. They can be summarised as follows:

- Student-centred teaching, which requires students to be trained how to learn independently.

- A teacher role that is totally unlike the traditional role, which focuses on teaching contents. The new role is that of managing students' learning process.

- Competence-based learning.

- Changes in how learning is organised, a curricular working perspective that reinforces continuity and coordination.

- A conceptual reorganisation of the educational role of universities in order to adapt to the new models of lifelong learning (LLL).

- New functionality of teaching materials, which become resources capable of generating high-level knowledge and facilitating independent learning. Information and communication technologies are key allies on this point.

- A new approach to assessment that is integrated into the learning activities and used strategically.

- The use of ECTS credits as a tool for curriculum-building.

The use of credits that are conceptually equal throughout the entire EU will also mean the use of grades that are comparable among different systems (ECTS grades), as well as the spread of a working methodology that seeks comprehensive student education and working documents. This includes teaching guides, in which the universities provide detailed information on their degrees and services, models of certificates and the Diploma Supplement as the standardised end document that should summarise all the most important information on what the student has studied. This Diploma Supplement seeks international transparency and the deserved academic and professional recognition of degrees. The goal is to provide a description of the nature, level, context, content and rank of studies undertaken by the holder of the original degree to which the supplement is attached.

The university of the twenty-first century is facing transcendental changes that translate into a twofold opportunity which Agustín Lacruz (2008: 28) aptly describes. First, we must reflect on the role of education within the Information and Knowledge Society, as an institution that generates, transmits, promotes and communicates knowledge; in parallel, we must conscientiously analyse the contents, forms and methods of teaching and learning used to achieve its goals.

Society asks universities not only for rigorous scientific research but also for an active quest for quality teaching, and it requires faculty to approach education from a more pedagogical perspective that generates learning. There is no question that this new educational approach entails shifting from a model focused on the faculty's teaching activities, which is grounded upon teaching and contents, to a different model focused on independent student learning and competence-based learning, a core notion in the model set forth in the EHEA.

Competence-based education has arisen from the need to go beyond the simplistic approach of teaching for instrumental qualification, that is, in order to do something better. Today's professional needs multiple skill sets, cultures, virtues and values on employment that are part and parcel of their personal and civic development, technical and humanistic training. Competences are linked to professional performance, to the activities this entails and, in short, to the problems professionals grapple with. Competence is always expressed in qualified, contextualised knowledge in a specific situation.

To this we must add the rising demand for constant, permanent, lifelong learning within the context of the Knowledge Society and the globalised economy. Learning how to learn and learning one's whole life in a society subjected to increasingly quick changes is the most important, useful and necessary competence of all. The competences of learning how to learn, of independent learning, of learning with others and of forming learning and practice communities is a totally new chapter in the book of human education and learning.

All of this is leading to a profound change, a global approach to learning. The ECTS credits, which measure students' efforts, are focused on learning and achieving well-defined objectives. The higher or lower quality of a course does not come from more or fewer hours taught but from the student's ability to assimilate the teaching-learning units with a critical capacity to analyse and synthesise. This system entails acceptance of the Nordic or Anglo-Saxon model, which revolves around student learning as opposed to today's continental Napoleonic model, which regards the contents transmitted by the educator as the crux of education.

The adoption of the European credit system involves not just a method for quantifying learning but also the choice of an underlying philosophy based on the student workload, which implies a new approach to teaching methods in higher education. What matters now is not knowledge in and of itself but effective learning. The educational model being promoted by the European Union revolves around student learning, as students must be given the competences that allow them to learn how to learn. It is based on the Nordic or Anglo-Saxon model of education, which aims to ensure that education extends over a citizen's entire lifetime (lifelong learning). To accomplish this, students must be given skills that encompass basic, generic, transversal and more specific competences. The model being posited is based on a belief that knowledge is meaningless without the corresponding competences, as competences are not just resources but also processes in which each individual puts their knowledge into action in a different way.

This model seems to adapt to today's Knowledge Society, which is flexible and ever-changing and requires creativity, improvisation and evolution in professional skills. It is an educational prototype that stands in stark contrast to the continental or Napoleonic model, which is grounded on contents and corresponds to the industrial society, characterised by closely guided activity, the absence of improvisation and a lack of evolution in professional skills.

The greater weight that education must attribute to students' independent learning demands new approaches to teaching and student work that will foster the role libraries play in universities. They will have to expand and converge with other services, chiefly with IT but also with multimedia production services, career orientation and information services, language services, and others.

At a time when traditional classroom teaching is losing ground to education based on student learning, university leaders must consider the prominent, dynamic role that libraries should take on when implementing the ECTS. One of the main cornerstones of the new orientation in the teaching-learning circuit, which will largely be supported by the new model of university library, will be the electronic resources available in learning and research resource centres, which we shall examine in the next chapter.

In the new educational model, libraries will have to participate in creating learning environments, contribute to drawing up teaching resources, take part in innovation groups and serve as the main support. In short, they will have to become dynamic places that encompass all the resources that support learning and research at the university.

E-Research and e-Science

Electronic publishing is an uncontested reality in developed countries. Scientific e-journals successfully paved the way, driven by the need for instantaneous information dissemination coupled with their extraordinary ability to adapt to researchers' needs. The backdrop is the process of globalisation and the internationalisation of knowledge. The scientific model of communication entrenched in printed publications was shattered in the digital, interconnected world.

Furthermore, the dawning of the new century meant the joint mobilisation of the academic and library communities in the quest for a new model under the heading of open access, which aims to overcome the restrictive control imposed by the publishers of scientific journals. As Carr (2007: 159) concludes, even though much remains to be done before a viable model of scientific communication and research emerges, the pressure for change and the intelligence of the research community itself seem to be enough reason to trust that solutions will be found and the power of the networks will ultimately be properly used to facilitate academic communication on a new, much more effective basis.

Likewise, after several shaky years, all indications seem to point to the emergence of the e-book as an indisputable fact today. The growth in production and demand for e-books has risen steadily, leading the American Publishers Association to state (2009): 'E-books saw a 23.6 percent increase from last year with $67 million in sales and a compound growth rate of 55.7 percent since 2002. E-books continue to grow significantly, sales reached $113 million in 2008, up 68.4%'.

Inevitably, as Webb et al. (2007: 125) point out, library services and resources have evolved and changed in response to the shifts in research needs, as well as to external factors such as changes in information technologies and in university education in general. The library and its professionals, they add, will be responsible for ensuring that the research community is as well informed as possible. In order to provide twenty-first century researchers with a suitable service, libraries need to ask their patrons what they want from the library and combine the results of these surveys with new ideas and developments, serve as support for research groups and poise themselves within the research community at a time when technological advances proliferate and the new concept of e-Science has been coined.

E-Science is a new way of researching that can be described as revolutionary. It is sustained on the generation of repositories and the development of infrastructures to analyse and share information among researchers living in different places. E-Science offers scientists in each discipline a different way to conduct their research. The key seems to lie in coordinating efforts within a national framework in order to generate comprehensive, viable solutions that cover researchers' information needs. Carr (2007: 169) believes that the challenge of e-Science is perhaps the most significant test facing research libraries to emerge in the last decade.

Borgman (2008) clarifies that e-Science is characterised by data-intensive, information-intensive, distributed, interdisciplinary and collaborative research. Scholars in all fields are taking advantage of new sources of data and new means to publish and distribute their work online. No longer are data considered interim products to be discarded once the research reporting them is published. Rather, they have become important sources of scholarly content to be used and reused. As the demand for curation of research data accelerates, data repositories may become the new special collections for research libraries. The advent of e-Science presents an array of challenges and responsibilities for libraries, such as scalable and sustainable infrastructure, open access to publications and data, and policies for access to data and computational resources.

Even though several countries with high research capital, such as the Netherlands and Finland, have pursued national solutions to the problems mentioned, the United Kingdom has managed to combine all the considerations involved in distributing scientific contents. Since 2001, the British scientific community, through the Research Support Libraries Group (RSLG),[8] has been recommending that a new national organisation be created to provide strategic leadership in the realm of research library development. This organisation will be called the Research Information Network (RIN).[9] The purpose of this organisation is to issue recommendations for creating an overall strategic framework in the United Kingdom that sets up coordinated mechanisms for providing scientific information which ensures that researchers will continue to have access to all the information resources regardless of their location.

In the United States, the Association of Research Libraries (ARL) Joint Task Force on Library Support for E-Science released an Agenda for Developing E-Science in Research Libraries (2007). The report concluded that ARL's engagement in the issues of e-Science is best focused on educational and policy roles, while partnering with other relevant organisations to contribute in strategic areas of technology development and new genres of publication. These types of strategic collaborations will also provide opportunities to re-envision the research library's role and contribution as twenty-first century science takes shape.

The 2004 White Paper on e-Science in Spain[10] published by the Spanish Foundation for Science and Technology defines e-Science as all scientific activities conducted through the use of resources accessible on the Internet. The evolution in high-speed communication networks devoted to research, along with collaborative technologies and applications, is creating the ideal setting for interaction among researchers. For this reason, as the document points out, even though e-Science can be conducted individually, it is more effective when joined with global partnering.

The research community is facing major challenges that necessitate access to multiple resources, as well as the need for infrastructures that facilitate knowledge sharing and collaboration. IT has a vast capacity for calculation and data storage, but specialised instrumental use, access to simulation and visualisation resources, database inquiries and access to collaborative applications, as well as other resources are needed to address these scientific challenges.

The taxonomy of e-Science has been depicted by three horizontal layers representing accessible resources (calculation, storage, information and other resources); communication networks, which provide access to these resources; and middleware or intermediate software. This last layer allows the applications to use the resources available at remote locations either jointly or in coordination.

The development of e-Science is instrumental in determining scientific and technological capacity in a globalised economy. Information provision is one of the essential infrastructures in the culture of research. Access to digital contents is top priority in any national science policy, and it must be spearheaded by the libraries, an institution with a tradition of organising and disseminating contents.

We agree with Carr (2007: 179) that the big question of research libraries' future role in supporting science in the digital environment is whether they can convince the e-Science communities that they are able to bring added value to the new research activity. Libraries must be effectively included on the agendas of research councils, must convince scientists that they are crucial partners in this enterprise and must have the political skills needed to successfully take part in the breakneck pace of e-Science development.

Innovative academic libraries in the Knowledge Society

Recent studies on the behaviour of university library patrons in the past few years are striking. The CIBER study (2008) commissioned by the British Library and the Joint Information Systems Committee (JISC) on the behaviour of future researchers stresses the urgent importance that libraries understand the behaviours of today's patrons in a hybrid library. It also states that academic and research libraries offer a huge volume of valuable contents, but often through systems that seem less intuitive than the ubiquitous search engines.

According to the conclusions of a report promoted by OCLC (De Rosa et al., 2006) which analyses the results of a survey administered between May and June 2005 to university students from 396 schools in six different countries, search engines are the favoured tool for starting an information search (89 per cent), compared to just 2 per cent who use the library website. Likewise, even though 41 per cent of the respondents do use the library website, only 10 per cent agreed that it meets their information needs.

Many university students make no distinction whatsoever between what libraries offer and what commercial search engines offer. They show identical trust in the results from both systems, and they view libraries as synonymous with books without necessarily identifying these institutions as crucial agents in information provision. The challenge, as the OCLC report concludes, is to define and clearly publicise the paramount role of the library in the infosphere.

Both studies agree that students prefer a general search in Google over a more sophisticated search that requires more time in the library. Plus, they demand not only quick responses but also responses that include a complete text.

Along these lines, Byrum (2005) stresses that it is imperative to implement initiatives that bolster the contents of bibliographic records and links from them to other electronic resources so that libraries can hold on to their leadership in information provision in the electronic age. In the past decade, the search for information has been irremediably conditioned by online search engines (Byrum, 2005), and libraries have not yet responded adequately to their patrons' needs.

Some of the trends identified in the recent report drawn up by the Web Services Steering Committee at the University of Minnesota Libraries dovetail with these findings, and we believe that their recommendations bear repetition (Hanson et al., 2009: 24), particularly the two below:

- Discovery should be organised around users rather than collections or systems. This organisation should be based on realistic, evidence-based models of our users and their research tasks.

- Users are successfully discovering relevant resources through non-library systems (e.g. general web searches, e-commerce sites and social networking applications). We need to ensure that items in our collections and licensed resources are discoverable in non-library environments.

The exhaustive study by the ACRL Research Committee (2008) points to trends which should be regarded as top priority. The study indicates that most of the survey respondents agreed that higher education will be increasingly viewed as a business, and that calls for accountability and for quantitative measures of library contributions to the research, teaching and service missions of the institution will shape library assessment programmes and approaches to the allocation of institutional resources. Likewise, most respondents agreed with this assumption: As part of the 'business of higher education', students will increasingly view themselves as 'customers' of the academic library and will demand high-quality facilities, resources and services attuned to their needs and concerns.

The roles played by research support librarians proposed by Webb et al. (2007: 141–5) fit in with these points:

- Gatekeeper: someone who filters through key information.

- Translator: librarian who tries to make our systems easy to use and, failing that, to support people in their use.

- Information specialist: expert at finding information, resources and data. Confident users of resources in our specialist areas.

- Subject expert: active researcher, developing an empathy with your subject and building up your role as an authority on library provision to support it.

- 'Safe harbour': make your researchers feel welcome when they visit or contact you.

- 'The fount of all knowledge': the main interface between researchers and the library service.

- 'A counsel, colleague and critical friend': shift from being seen as a support assistant to a valued and trusted colleague.

All of these lead to a reinforcement of the idea that libraries must avoid inertia and instead adopt a proactive role that can respond to the university community's needs in advance. The new model of higher education and the challenges posed by e-Science require librarians to not only support but also foster learning and research. To do this, they need acceptance by patrons, recognition of the services they provide and the university community's active participation.

Notes

1. Sorbonne Joint Declaration: Joint declaration on harmonisation of the architecture of the European higher education system by the four ministers in charge for France, Germany, Italy and the United Kingdom, Paris, the Sorbonne, 25 May 1998. *http://www.eees.es/pdf/Sorbona_EN.pdf*

2. The Bologna Declaration: Joint declaration of the European Ministers of Education. Bologna, 19 June 1999. *http://www.bologna-bergen2005.no/Docs/00-Main_doc/990719BOLOGNA_DECLARATION.PDF*

3. Communiqué of the meeting of European Ministers in charge of Higher Education in Prague: 'Towards the European Higher Education Area'. Prague, 19 May 2001. *http://www.bologna-bergen2005.no/Docs/00-Main_doc/010519PRAGUE_COMMUNIQUE.PDF*

4. Communiqué of the Conference of Ministers responsible for Higher Education in Berlin: 'Realising the European Higher Education Area'. Berlin, 19 September 2003. *http://www.bologna-bergen2005.no/Docs/00-Main_doc/030919Berlin_Communique.PDF*

5. Communiqué of the Conference of European Ministers Responsible for Higher Education in Bergen: 'The European Higher Education Area – Achieving the Goals'. Bergen, 19–20 May 2005. *http://www.bologna-bergen2005.no/Docs/00-Main_doc/050520_Bergen_Communique.pdf*

6. London communiqué: 'Towards the European Higher Education Area: Responding to Challenges in a Globalised World'. London, 18 May 2007. *http://www.dfes.gov.uk/londonbologna/uploads/documents/LC18May07.pdf*

7. Communiqué of the Conference of European Ministers Responsible for Higher Education in Leuven/ Louvain-la-Neuve: 'The Bologna Process 2020 – The European Higher Education Area in the New Decade', 28–29 April 2009. *http://www.ond.vlaanderen.be/hogeronderwijs/bologna/conference/documents/Leuven_Louvain-la-Neuve_Communiqué_April_2009.pdf*

8. *http://www.rslg.ac.uk/*

9. *http://www.rin.ac.uk/*
10. *http://www.fecyt.es/fecyt/docs/tmp/-1870746289.pdf*

References

ACRL Research Committee (2008) *Environmental Scan 2007.* Chicago, IL: Association of College & Research Libraries. Available from: *http://www.acrl.org/ala/mgrps/divs/acrl/publications/whitepapers/Environmental_Scan_2007%20FINAL.pdf.*

Agustín Lacruz, M.C. (2008) 'El contexto educativo: el Espacio Europeo de Educación Superior y la innovación en las metodologías docentes', in M.C. Agustín Lacruz (coord.), *Diseño curricular y Guías docentes ECTS: Desde la Diplomatura de Biblioteconomía y Documentación hasta el Grado en Información y Documentación.* Zaragoza: Prensas Universitarias de Zaragoza, pp. 21–37.

American Publishers Association (AAP) (2009) *Industry Statistics.* Available from: *http://www.publishers.org/main/IndustryStats/indStats_02.htm.*

Association of Research Libraries (ARL) (2007) *Agenda for Developing E-Science in Research Libraries.* Available from: *http://www.arl.org/bm~doc/ARLESciencefinal.pdf.*

Borgman, C.L. (2008) 'The role of libraries in e-science', in *The 11th European Conference of Medical and Health Libraries, Helsinki, Finland, 23–28 June 2008, Towards a New Information Space – Innovations and Renovations.* Available from: *http://www.terkko.helsinki.fi/bmf/EAHILppt/Christine_L_Borgman.pdf.*

Byrum, J.D. (2005) 'Recommendations for urgently needed improvement of OPAC and the role of the National Bibliographic Agency in achieving it', in *71st IFLA*

General Conference and Council. Available from: *http://www.ifla.org/IV/ifla71/papers/124e-Byrum.pdf.*

Carr, R. (2007) *The Academic Research Library in a Decade of Change.* Oxford: Chandos.

CIBER (Centre for Information Behaviour and the Evaluation of Research) (2008) *Information Behaviour of the Researcher of the Future.* London: School of Library, Archive and Information Studies, University College London. Available from: *http://www.ucl.ac.uk/infostudies/research/ciber/downloads/ggexecutive.pdf.*

De Rosa, C. et al. (2006) *College Students' Perceptions of Libraries and Information Resources: A Report to the OCLC Membership.* Dublin, OH: OCLC. Available from: *http://www.oclc.org/reports/pdfs/studentperceptions.pdf.*

Hanson, C. et al. (2009) *Discoverability: Phase 1, Final Report.* University of Minnesota Libraries. Available from: *http://conservancy.umn.edu/handle/48258.*

Webb, J., Gannon-Leary, P. and Bent, M. (2007) *Providing Effective Library Services for Research.* London: Facet.

3

Academic libraries over the last few years

From the start, university libraries have been a priority service within the university which ensures that the institution they serve carries out the teaching and research entrusted to it. The existence of the library is therefore justified as a service to support the university in fulfilling its goals, and for this reason the library must be effectively integrated into the university's institutions.

This integration bears a direct relationship with the importance of the library within the institutions. This can be seen in the specific rules governing the library, the financial resources earmarked for it, the library's inclusion in the university's strategic plans and its participation in the institution's governing bodies.

Right now, immersed as we are in the Knowledge Society, the university is called upon to play a leading role in the training of citizens and in the production, transmission and dissemination of knowledge. As a support for the university, university libraries must become the backbone of the processes of learning and research. The UNESCO report entitled *Towards Knowledge Societies* (2005: 66–7) stresses that 'the future of libraries hinges largely on the capacity of our societies to transcend the mercantile logic of information society and to install new models in which what creates value is knowledge and the value of its contribution to cognition ... The library will remain a pillar of the social circulation of knowledge and a factor of vitality for learning networks. Is it not, with its cognitive and evolutive functions, the paradigm of the learning organization?'

University libraries are facing drastic changes in the expectations that students, educators and researchers have regarding access to information resources that support learning, teaching and research. We agree with Rowley and Roberts (2009: 197) that information professionals have no other choice but to constantly change; not only do they need to respond to the transformations in users' expectations, they must also work in tandem with other academic services and professional groups, even though this might go beyond the traditional concept of the library, to create new models of holistic support for students and new environments for teaching-learning and to aid in research.

Hybrid libraries

The wholesale inclusion of information technologies into libraries has turned academic collections into hybrid collections, in which traditional formats exist side by side with digital collections from a variety of sources, including the institution's historical collections that have been digitalised; repositories of digital documents, mainly teaching or research materials generated by the university itself; and electronic resources, most of them through subscriptions with the commercial suppliers of scientific contents.

Orera (2005) claims that the new model of hybrid university library has the following features:

- It is a new kind of library, as it entails a profound transformation in what services it offers, how they are provided, etc.

- It is characterised by selecting, processing and disseminating information in both printed and digital forms. The traditional function of owning information has been joined by management of access to information housed in remote servers. In addition, the amount and proportion of digital information in the collections has risen steadily. There is total permeability between printed and digital documents.

- The entire library management relies on IT, the use of the Internet and the use of web technologies.

- Patron services are provided both at the library's physical site and virtually, leading many of these services to no longer be constrained by time. The inclusion of remote users means a diversification and multiplication of users in a new context in which user training takes on paramount importance.

- The university library shoulders new functions. Worth stressing is the library's new role as a publisher of teaching and research materials.

- The complexity of managing hybrid collections demands information professionals with sound IT skills and multidisciplinary, qualified training. The constant changes taking place in the Knowledge Society in which the library is immersed demand proactive professionals who constantly receive further training.

- The hybrid library solves traditional problems like a lack of coordination. The university library is an information system with common goals for the entire university. In addition to library policy, other contributors include the use of TCP/IP technologies, which make remote work possible, the optimisation of intranets and the crucial importance of the library's website in offering patron services in a uniform way.

- There is a rise in cooperation among librarians and the essential role of consortia both in the purchase of licences for databases, journals and electronic books and in aspects related to interlibrary loans, publishing statistical reports and ongoing training of professionals in the member libraries.

- Attention must be paid to new technical problems like the preservation of digital information and copyright protection.

Claims Brophy (2005: 52):

> it seems highly unlikely that the undoubted benefits of the electronic or digital model will enable it to become dominant in the foreseeable future. Not only does the traditional, largely print-based model have several advantages, but there is an enormous investment in 'legacy systems' content and infrastructure, including systems for publishing content in traditional forms, which have been built up over many years and which retain immense value. For all these reasons, it is likely that for the foreseeable future academic libraries will operate on the hybrid model.

In our opinion, we are in the midst of a transition in which the changes are taking place at breakneck speed, leading us to a more or less distant future in which the university library will eventually have to be a digital library.

From libraries to Learning Resource Centres

As mentioned above, universities are required to adapt to the changes that society and learning impose. University libraries, as a prominent part of this system, will have to change and remodel their approach. They will have to have a flexible functional structure that enables resources and information services to be managed regardless of their medium or location, and they will have to provide appropriate access to these resources with no temporal or spatial constraints. In order to adapt to this new context, the university library must go one step further to become a learning and research resource centre (Pinto et al., 2008: 30).

Taking as our point of departure the Information Commons in the United States and the Integrated Learning Resources Centres of the United Kingdom, the Spanish Network of University Libraries (Area, 2005: 21) suggests interpreting what are called Learning and Research Resource Centres as dynamic settings which bring together all the resources that support learning and research at the university under one roof. They are therefore university services whose goal is to help professors and students by facilitating their learning, education, management and problem-solving in the access and use of information, regardless of whether these activities are technical, methodological or knowledge-based.

The essential circumstances that have led to the advent of this kind of centre include:

- the emergence of the Knowledge Society;
- the revamping of teaching methods that stress learning as opposed to teaching;
- the demand for quality in university services;
- the potential of the new technologies;
- lifelong learning;
- economy of resources;
- competition among universities.

The conception of a library as a repository of documents waiting to be consulted is a far cry from this new model, which is a centre that anticipates and generates patrons' potential needs. The core around which it revolves is not books or documents but the patrons themselves.

Martínez (2003) listed the following key concepts of Learning Resource Centres (LRCs) as follows, and we concur:

- The LRC is a new model of university library. As it is prepared to handle the current and future changes in the world of learning, it can serve as a major springboard within the university itself to successfully achieve the transformations that must be implemented as part of the new European Higher Education Area (EHEA).

- The LRC is a model of library envisioned to support a new teaching philosophy based on innovation and improved learning quality, on the transformation of the associated methods and practices and on a change in the role of the main players in the educational process: professors and students.

- The LRC is a model of university library based on a new conception and organisation of university services. Integrating services, working towards the same objectives, being accountable, showing results and improving patrons' satisfaction are the strands that result in a new university organisation.

- The LRC is a model of university library that neither exhausts nor eliminates other current or future models. It must be applied after an analysis of the different services offered by the university as a whole or a given campus. LRCs can coexist alongside other libraries in the school, faculty or department, yet they are always integrated into this dynamic and not divorced from it.

- The LRC is a model of academic library that makes it possible for librarians to perform new professional roles. It is more important and enriching for the librarian to work alongside other university professionals and become a key actor in the development of new educational projects.

The Network of Spanish University Libraries (REBIUN) has laid down the following four strands of the LRC as summarised in Figure 3.1.

Potential services offered by Learning Resource Centres

The activities performed at LRCs are designed to achieve the following objectives:

- To attain quality products and services for a wide variety of students, professors and researchers.
- To train a staff of professionals who are capable of helping patrons make the most of the resources and services provided.

Figure 3.1   Key concepts of an LRC

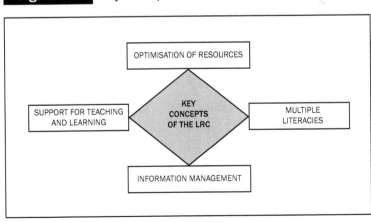

Source: Area (2005: 22).

- To offer a dynamic, flexible setting for lifelong learning.

LRCs entail a convergence of services. Taking advantage of synergies and moving towards a new educational model focused on learning make it necessary to evolve in this direction. Balagué Mola (2003) uses the following arguments to defend the convergence of services as the key factor in creating LRCs:

- All university services share a mission: to support teaching, learning and research. Therefore, the LRC makes a decisive contribution to the university's mission.

- The new educational paradigm makes universities reconsider not only teaching but also all the elements that support it. As a result, LRCs contribute to innovation in teaching.

- The range of possibilities offered by the new information technologies is vast and constantly changing. The convergence of services within the LRC enables the university to devise a shared strategy for information management.

- The convergence of services can serve to provide better assistance to students, professors and researchers, who only have a single service as their interlocutor. LRCs enable users to be offered concentrated, higher quality services more aligned with their needs.

- The very existence of the basic structures of different services prompts a certain degree of duplication, and convergence can help to cut costs, especially if the complementary services are all housed in a single building, which also tends to have a more extensive timetable. In this way, resources are optimised and bureaucracy is lowered.

- Multimedia technology, a result of the integration of different media (images, motion, video, voice, text, graphics and other computerised data) has become a key factor in education, learning and information, and therefore in library services.

- In addition to a challenge, convergence can also serve as an incentive for communication among professionals from different fields (librarians, academic staff specialising in educational design, graphic designers, analysts and programmers, systems and database administrators, publishers, printers, video and audio producers, copyright experts, administrative staff and other kinds of support staff).

- The LRC can be a steady ally of lifelong learning. European convergence means not just more facilities for cooperation but also a rise in competition among universities. Future students will weigh the quality of teaching when choosing a university, but they will also take other added values into account, such as the learning support tools available.

With regard to the relations between traditional library services and other university services, the results of a survey conducted by Balagué Mola (2003) with Spanish university libraries are insightful. The survey revealed that the greatest cooperation is forged between library services and IT services (81 per cent), while cooperation between library services and educational institutes (35 per cent) and digital teacher support services (35 per cent) is much lower. Meanwhile, cooperation with institutional information services (16 per cent) is negligible. Generally speaking, librarians see greater convergence as a positive step, although there is also some reluctance with regard to the cost that this convergence entails in terms of flexibility.

Learning Resource Centres are more than just a physical or virtual place housing certain resources related to the distribution and organisation of information. The most important part is not their appearance (centralised, decentralised or blended models) but the convergence of services they offer. We cannot say that one organisational model is better than the other, as it depends on the characteristics and specific needs of each university.

Even though there are quite exhaustive classifications of the possible services that an LRC can provide (Martínez, 2003), below is a summary of the six categories outlined by Pinto et al. (2008: 73–81):

1. *Library and documentation services.* An LRC can offer basic learning services and library services for research and lifelong learning.

2. *Information and communication.* This service channels the flows of information by designing its own consistent information systems for taking decisions.

3. *Technology.* This includes developing university management and administration, implementing library applications and designing strategies and programmes for e-learning platforms, virtual classrooms or research platforms, as well as support for the creation of contents and IT training for faculty.

4. *Language service.* Translation and proofreading services, development of multilingual materials, language self-study areas, coordination and training for foreign students or exchange faculty.

5. *Multimedia production service.* Support for the design and production of multimedia resources: videos, tutorials, portals, learning materials, etc. This requires cooperation with the innovation, education, library and IT services. It

is crucial to use standards like XML, SCORM, metadata, etc., which make it possible to integrate these multimedia products into e-learning platforms, as well as to recover and reuse them.

6. *Innovation and learning service.* A transversal service focusing on teaching innovation projects, faculty training activities, etc.

Benefits of Learning Resource Centres for their users

The driving forces behind LRCs are users' requirements and needs, and their goal is to improve the quality of the teaching-learning processes and the research output of the university community. LRCs are designed so that the end users receive top-notch service.

Below is a list by Martínez (2003) of the benefits that LRCs offer their users:

- Increased use of resources that the university allocates to its users. Users find everything in an integrated way.

- Improvement in the quality of the educational model through library information sources which are both physically present and electronic. Users receive quality.

- Better awareness of the academic community's real learning and research needs. Users communicate their range of needs.

- Rationalisation of a single physical space by offering a variety of services that used to be commonly found dispersed over different campuses and faculties or schools. Users know what resources are available.

- Integration of educational technologies and ICTs in the same place, whereas today they are often dispersed. This integration provides the entire community with the same level of services and access. Users use the resources properly and feel satisfied.

- Increase in the use of the resources and services meant for users, without having to go anywhere. Users come out ahead and make better use of the time they spend on managing their learning.

- Improvement in the quality of university social life and its milieu. Users experience the university and the academic spirit more intensely.

- Better use of and freeing up of spaces and resources in the faculties and schools, which can be assigned to other university projects. Users also have more resources and services at their disposal.

- Merger of all the 'non-curricular' training available at the university. Users can choose better and receive higher quality.

- Reorganisation, rationalisation and better use of the resources, especially human resources, which used to be dispersed and assigned to different services. Users feel better served.

- A wide range of services can be offered in more extensive timetables planned by the users. Users can organise themselves better.

- Provision of spaces and cooperation programmes with institutions and companies in the environs. Users can see the institution's relationship with its immediate environs and region.

We can say that this is a chance to make the most of the synergies among the different services with the goal of creating one that is more than the mere sum of its components. It is an alternative that adapts to the new teaching-learning models demanded by today's society which each university can adapt to their own particular needs, structure and budget.

As an example, we can cite several outstanding models, like the Library and Learning Centre at the University of Bath,[1] the Dublin City University Library[2] and the Library and Learning Center of the University of Wisconsin[3] in the United States. In Spain, worth spotlighting is the experiment launched in academic year 2002–3 by the Polytechnic University of Catalonia, The Teaching Resources Factory (Figure 3.2),[4] a service to create and develop electronic teaching resources which is supported by a specialised team of librarians, IT specialists and multimedia experts.

Redefining the concept of academic library

Above we have sketched out the new dynamic where university libraries need to channel their efforts. The challenge

Figure 3.2 The Teaching Resources Factory at the Polytechnic University of Catalonia

lies in grappling with the new changes and demands in order to turn the library into a catalyst of learning and research. Ignoring these needs may mean that libraries are definitively relegated to secondary or residual status, on the sidelines of the innovation being demanded of the university as a whole.

This seems totally congruent with the definition of university library proposed by REBIUN (Orera, 2005: 47):

> The library is a resource centre for learning, teaching and research and activities related to the operation and management of the university as a whole. The mission of the academic library is to provide access to and the dissemination of information resources and to participate in the processes of creating knowledge in order to contribute to achieving the institutional goals. It is the library's duty to choose and manage the different information resources regardless of their budgetary line item, where they were acquired or their material support.

Institutions that choose to undertake these changes must transform the library utilising a new approach: by coming up with a new design of its spaces and services to bring together other elements that used to be outside the library; by equipping and defining appropriate furnishings that are adapted not only to books but also work stations, thus ensuring access to digital information; by providing all kinds of hardware and software; by implementing extensive timetables; by providing other diversified materials and resources; and by defining a new organisation and new procedures (Martínez, 2003).

We believe that the 2007–10 strategic goals of the Network of Spanish Libraries, REBIUN (Red de Bibliotecas Universitarias, 2006) pursue this line, as they include the following:

- In the realm of learning:
  - To continue to foster the new model of university library as a Learning and Research Resource Centre.
  - To encourage and promote actions to develop and implement IT skills as a transversal competence within the new teaching model.
- In the realm of research:
  - To promote, enhance, exploit and improve digital library access, contents and services with the purpose of improving and enhancing the quality of research, development and innovation at Spanish libraries.
  - To guide, promote, coordinate and disseminate the new policies and projects on intellectual property in the realm of document loan services and in the new electronic and digital environment.
- In the realm of quality:
  - To promote, disseminate, lead and share evaluation processes in order to improve, ensure and raise the quality of library services, as well as the efficacy and efficiency of the resources allocated and the institution's accountability.
  - To continue to conduct joint actions in order to improve and increase the professionalism of the people working at university libraries in view of the new challenges facing universities.

We recommend a careful look at the results and conclusions from the project currently underway entitled 'Vision for the academic libraries and information services of the future (September 2009–April 2011)'.[5] The project partners are the British Library, Joint Information Systems Committee (JISC), Research Information Network (RIN), Research Libraries

UK (RLUK) and the Society of College, National and University Libraries (SCONUL).

The purpose of the project is to explore the challenges faced by higher education and libraries to facilitate strategic planning. It will help higher education institutions and organisations to look at the challenges faced from a fresh focus and formulate strategies to ensure that the sector continues to be a leading global force. Libraries are fundamental to learning, teaching and research. But the world is changing; factors such as the digital revolution, the knowledge economy, students and researchers as 'consumers' and the global economic crisis are transforming the landscape. What will be the information needs of users?

Notes

1. *http://www.bath.ac.uk/library/*
2. *http://www.library.dcu.ie/tour/ground3.html*
3. *http://www.uwstout.edu/lib/tour/index.htm*
4. *http://www.upc.edu/factoria/*
5. *http://www.futurelibraries.info/content/*

References

Area, M. (ed.) (2005) *De las bibliotecas universitarias a los centros de recursos para el aprendizaje y la investigación.* Madrid: CRUE.

Balagué Mola, N. (2003) 'La biblioteca universitaria, centro de recursos para el aprendizaje y la investigación: Una aproximación al estado de la cuestión en España', in *II Jornadas Rebiun: Los Centros de Recursos para el Aprendizaje y la Investigación en los procesos de innovación docente.* Palma de Mallorca: REBIUN. Red de Bibliotecas

Universitarias. Available from: *http://150.244.9.206/sc/ documentos/Jornadas_REBIUN/3%20-%20biblioteca_ universitaria_CRAI.pdf.*

Brophy, P. (2005) *The Academic Library*, 2nd edn. London: Facet.

Martínez, D. (2003) 'El Centre de Recursos per a l'Aprenentatge (CRA): Un nou model de biblioteca universitària en l'era del coneixement', *Item: Revista de Biblioteconomia i Documentació*, 35: 35–54.

Orera, L. (ed.) (2005) *La Biblioteca universitaria: Concepto, funciones y retos futuros*. La biblioteca universitaria, Madrid: Síntesis, pp. 19–49.

Pinto, M., Sales, D. and Osorio, P. (2008) *Biblioteca universitaria, CRAI y alfabetización informacional*. Gijón: Trea.

REBIUN (Red de Bibliotecas Universitarias) (2006) *II Plan Estratégico 2007–2010*. Available from: *http://www. rebiun.org/doc/plan.pdf.*

Rowley, J. and Roberts, S. (2009) 'Influential leadership for academic libraries', in J.R. Griffiths and J. Crave (eds), *Access, Delivery, Performance: The Future of Libraries without Walls*. London: Facet, pp. 197–214.

UNESCO (2005) *Towards Knowledge Societies*. Available from: *http://unesdoc.unesco.org/images/0014/001418/ 141843e.pdf.*

4

The challenge of enhancing traditional services

Catalogues

Three decades of online catalogues

The current framework in which the information search and retrieval develops has triggered irreversible changes, both in the function traditionally assigned to the online catalogues and in the position that they occupy in access to information, in competition with the collection of global tools for retrieval implemented in the web. It seems clear that nowadays catalogues do not represent nuclear elements in the information search and that they have to limit themselves to occupy a modest second level.

Originally, the online catalogue was conceived as an essential library tool and we think that, to a certain extent, this conception of the OPAC has survived on the part of the professional community which has considered the catalogue as a product of the technical processes of the library rather than as a service to the user, a user immersed in the information society and that seems to demand very different online catalogues from those provided nowadays.

Libraries, and specifically university libraries, have made huge investments in order to adapt to the technological changes required by the web, placing particular emphasis on interoperability and standardisation. However, resources, library services and Information and Documentation professionals seem, in a way, to go unnoticed in the universe of superabundance of information that characterises our society and to hold a marginal position in the consumer market of electronic information.

Apart from modifying almost every technical task in the centres, the Internet has brought about one of the main challenges the professionals face at this moment: the incorporation of traditional and electronic, physical and virtual information, in fee and under licence information. Paradoxically we can notice two trends that affect the conception of the OPAC as a retrieval tool in the library: integration and diversification. As we have pointed out, on the one hand, the catalogue in the hybrid libraries includes books, e-books, printed and electronic journals, web resources, etc., and, on the other hand, from the library web portal the user may access databases subscribed to by the institution, platforms of electronic content providers, other catalogues, repositories and resources. This situation has an important level of complexity for the end user in order to understand the functionality and the added value of the OPAC in contrast to other retrieval tools, and to choose the online catalogue as the first search element, even in the library portal.

The different information units have articulated the solution from three essential non-exclusive patterns: the inclusion of resources in the catalogue, inserting the link in the field 856, the implementation of metasearch engines which allow the simultaneous and cross-reference search to different electronic resources, making good use of metadata, such as MetaLib[1] or Research Pro,[2] and finally, solutions with specific tools that make up a new interface dissociated from the OPAC, such as AquaBrowser,[3] based on concept maps, indexes automatically, presents the results in order of relevance and redirects the user to the precise source, both inside and outside the library system; moreover, it compares the search terms of a user to the metadata from his catalogue with the aim of creating visual maps of associations or views of fields of interest.

To all these things we have to add the settlement of the systems of quotation links which makes good use of the advantages of OpenURL and the technological solutions provided by some of the main industry companies, that have specific applications to solve the complex network of links established in the treatment of electronic resources SFX from ExLibris, WebBridge LR from Innovative Interfaces or Resolver for SirsiDynix[4] illustrate this type of tool.

In spite of all the efforts aimed at the development of new catalogues, the obvious technological developments introduced by the vendor companies of software intended for resource integration, the work of the library community in the design of the portals and the adaptation of the services provided, it is inevitable that users do not find the OPACs easy to use. The arguments explained before are taken up again by Borgman (1996) in his study from 1986 to confirm the clear difficulties in using the online catalogues a decade later. The improvements in the interfaces, according to Professor Borgman, have been superficial; they have not responded to the essential functionalities of the OPAC, whose search systems are designed for the professional librarians with a solid conceptual background in information retrieval. Bearing in mind all these problems, we shouldn't be surprised by the conclusions of the report of Calhoun et al. (2009: 51) in which significant differences are emphasised between the qualitative priorities established by the users and librarians in the use of the catalogue, as well as in the data that this must provide. Whereas the librarians' point of view still clings to the classical principles of information arrangement, the users' expectations are clearly influenced by the web tools and services at their disposal.

For Novotny (2004), the interest shown in the OPACs started to decline when the concern in the libraries at the end of the 1990s focused on the inclusion of electronic resources in the collections. In this period, a new generation of users has entered the university, hoping that the online catalogues function as a search engine. The strategy of the standard question entails looking for the keyword and, as Novotny adds with greater surprise, 'these users do not have too much curiosity to know how the catalogue works, make the least possible effort to formulate their search and do not understand the capacities of an OPAC'.

In order to understand what Karen Markey (2007) calls the 'fall from grace' of the catalogue, the author reviews the lost opportunities from the beginning of the 1980s until the Google era and of the projects of massive digitalisation. From the golden age of the catalogue in the 1980s we pass to recommendations suggested in the 1990s, which have not been dealt with suitably:

- To make the subject search easier, using post-Boolean probabilistic searches with automatic spell checking, weight of terms, smart stemming, relevance feedback and arrangement of the results by relevance ranking.

- To invigorate the decisions of users' selection in the catalogue, adding tables of contents and indexes.

- To reduce the volume of failed searches in certain subjects, adding full texts to the catalogue, such as journal and newspaper articles, encyclopaedias, theses, reports from the different administrations, etc.

- To increase the search strategies through classifications.

In the same work Karen Markey points out ten reasons, with which we fully agree, explaining why these suggestions have not been applied:

1. Obsession of library professionals with descriptive cataloguing.

2. The priorities of the technical services were focused on the retrospective cataloguing or authority control.

3. Dedication focused on the technical services in contrast to the need to promote services to the user.

4. Constant increase per item in the cost of cataloguing.

5. Failure of the research community to reach an agreement about the most urgent needs for catalogue improvement and about the solutions to be adopted to reduce the costs allocated to cataloguing.

6. Failure to act harmoniously in the system improvements.

7. Inflationary trend in the library budgets.

8. The cost in the development of collections and the resources allocated to the licenses of electronic contents that drive the growth of the *open access* movement.

9. High costs, generally technological, of the Integrated Library System (ILS).

10. Failure of the ILS vendors to make changes in the retrieval technology that respond appropriately to the system improvements. Marked lack of connection between the institutions and the market forces to converge in a direction that keeps the users alert to OPAC.

The Calhoun (2006) report, commissioned by the Library of Congress, emphasises how the users attribute to the catalogue the tendency to contain mainly references, with very little capacity to do full text searches. People being interviewed at work categorically agree that the catalogue does not constitute a priority search tool in the range of existing possibilities; what's more, the catalogue provides insufficient coverage in the universe of academic information. The users surveyed seem to answer clearly the question of catalogue integration with other information retrieval tools, being inclined to go for the inclusion of the library collections in Google.

The current catalogue covers an important core collection, especially books and journals, in printed and electronic format, but this collection is limited with respect to what students and teachers wish to find and use. In view of this weakness, the user appreciates Google and appreciates particularly the tool Google Books, a huge project which couldn't have been possible without the digitalisation agreements undertaken in collaboration with some of the most important libraries all over the world; in addition to these agreements the collaboration with OCLC is also a significant fact, specifically the link to the results of WorldCat,[5] also accessible from Yahoo, or in Spain the agreement with REBIUN (Red de Bibliotecas Universitarias)[6] since 2006, combining the results of the Google Books searches and the collective catalogue in this network. Opinion is largely in favour of incorporating the catalogues into web engines, one of the actions recommended by Markey (2007) or the CIBER study (2008).

In the same report by Calhoun (2006: 38) it is stressed that the catalogue interface, whether unique or collective, 'should be similar and work as Google'. Users expect instantaneous satisfaction and positive feedback from the systems that they use. Likewise, people being interviewed suggested the enrichment of the catalogue with cover pictures, reviews, tables of contents, etc. In the same way, new ideas were considered for the improvement of usability of the catalogue through the FRBR concepts, display techniques and interactive characteristics. More interactive catalogues were suggested which could offer RSS sources, social marking, etc.

In that respect the report on Libraries of the University of California (2005: 7) is conclusive: the current library catalogues are inadequately designed for the tasks of search, retrieval and selection in the growing pool of resources available in our libraries. They are better adapted to the siting and acquisition of known items and, both for librarians and users, the catalogue is only another option of access to our collections. They offer a fragmented group of systems in order to search published information, catalogues, databases, platforms of electronic journals, institutional repositories, etc., each of them with different tools for the identification and procurement of materials. For the user these distinctions are arbitrary; they seek only simplicity in the search and satisfaction in the answer.

Also recently the common aspects of the catalogues have been noticed with the successful model of virtual bookshop led by Amazon.[7] Functionalities that the users appreciate especially in Amazon must make us reflect. Zumer (2007) notes six Amazon characteristics entirely comparable to the OPACs: simplicity, picture of the cover, recommendations based on the tracking of the behaviour of users, reviews-recommendations made by the readers, arrangement of the results according to popularity and availability of the content, and full text search.

While the progress made is acceptable, and the technological improvements implemented in the OPACs are noteworthy, the reality shown in the above paragraphs reveals the difficulties of the online catalogues; the coincidence and persistence in the research results for almost three decades is an unquestionable fact: the end user finds it difficult to use the catalogues and, moreover, the success of the web has led to the decline and displacement of the OPAC as a first order element in information retrieval.

Framework for the development of the catalogues

Evolution in the Integrated Library Systems

Traditionally, the OPAC functionalities were directly related to the system of library management used, a linking adopted for a long time, which is refuted clearly in the report of the University of California Libraries (2005: 42) where it is pointed out as one of its basic principles 'to rethink the architecture of the system in order to approach it according to the services, and not to the systems', emphasising the fact that applications such as the OPAC cannot be determined by an ILS. The need to revise the viewpoint of the system architecture is emphasised, with a view to get applications defined by the services rendered to the users.

The middle of the 1990s is considered the transformation age for library management systems; for Rowley (1998) this is the transition moment from the third generation systems to those of the fourth generation, in parallel with web expansion and with unstoppable trend towards standardisation and interoperability.

At present the ILSs are based on the client/server architecture, use of non-proprietary operating systems which make interoperability feasible and the integration of different platforms in the same system. Generally, they are based on relational databases management systems and object-oriented programming languages, and both in large and in small systems the graphical interfaces and the multimedia environments have been consolidated. To the traditional modules the vendors have been adding a suite of applications that let the libraries discard out-of-date interfaces without having to change the whole system.

We think that at this moment there are two main challenges of the ILSs: managing electronic collections appropriately and improving the interfaces of the OPACs. Salse Rovira (2005) points out how the OPAC modules are the ones that show more variations recently in coordination with an important range of additional programmes. Since the adoption of the OPAC web at the end of the 1990s we have gone to an online catalogue which acts as an integrator of resources and that allows, among other functionalities: addition of enriched content to the bibliographical record, access to services of virtual reference, act as metasearch engine, integrate links or allow access through mobile devices.

The industry companies present constant developments and innovations with OPACs in which the influence of the generic search tools in the web can be perceived as an adaptation pattern to the user preferences for access to the information. In this way, simpler environments come up, the use of menus or the advanced search seems to have been pushed into the background, even in the university or specialised library catalogues, including advanced functionalities, arrangement of results according to relevance, faceted navigation, fuzzy technology, searches in natural language, etc.

AquaBrowser (see Figure 4.1) was the pioneering product in the development of new interfaces; for its part, Ex Libris launched Primo, Innovative Interfaces Encore, VTLS[8] introduced Visualizer, etc. The emergent open source products, with Koha[9] at the top, have to be added to the commercial products. We agree with interpretations such as those of Breeding (2008), for whom the library automatisation business based in proprietary software licences is broken, products have become much more mature and the number of implementations of ILS open source has grown considerably. In this sense the work by Garza (2009) documents the successful implementation of Drupal[10] and other public APIs

Figure 4.1   AquaBrowser Library© in Queens Library

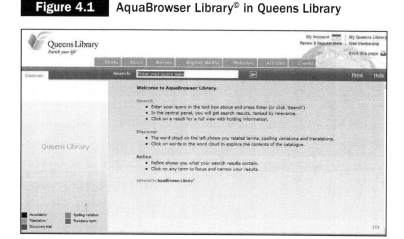

in an academic library, showing its integration with Millenium WebOpac, OCLC, LibraryThing, Google tools, etc.

In that respect special mention should be given to the eXtensible Catalog (XC)[11] project, hosted at the University of Rochester and funded from the Andrew W. Mellon Foundation Scholarly Communications Program, which is working to design and develop a set of open-source applications for libraries. At present they have two complete applications, whose source code is openly available. XC software is aimed at three areas: ILS and repository integration, metadata services and user interface. It is designed as a group of components rather than a monolithic traditional system, so the library will install the tool that fits its requirements.

One of the open discussions in the current literature focuses on the future role of the ILSs. On one hand, as Salse Rovira (2005) points out, we have the position of those who, like Borgman, defend the preservation of these systems, which will have to become more modular and fragmentary. On the other hand, authors such as Pace (2004) think that the ILSs as we know them today will tend to disappear, considering the possibility that the librarian selects the modules that better adapt to the centre, regardless of the vendor of these modules. In the same context, Tardón (2002: 269) suggests the need to redefine the ILSs operation; he adds that it is not enough to automatise technical tasks and offer collections to the users, it is necessary to increase the complexity of the information system and to develop this by means of the interconnection of information resources and the services with a view to optimise the efficiency of the resultant value chain. This trend seems to be endorsed by the designations themselves that this type of programme receives, now considered as applications platforms, rather than integrated systems; this is shown in labels, increasingly used, such as LMS (Library Management System) or LAF (Library Application Framework).

The report by JISC and SCONUL (2008) discusses a totally consolidated market, which tries to compete with services such as Google or Amazon, being focused on fostering the added value that their ILSs may provide to the libraries, observing the standards and pursuing interoperability. We consider that, specifically, the online catalogues and the related applications will benefit from being more receptive to the open source software, interfaces non-dependent on the system and a line of work aimed at adding value to the library data, moving away from the 'simple' lists of results and details of bibliographical records in order to move the collections from the hybrid libraries to the user environment.

Initiatives in the field of bibliographic information display

The study of the OPACs and the behaviour of the users constitute one of the richest and most prolific research areas and undoubtedly its results have benefitted the continuous evolution and improvement of the systems. García López (2007: 20–3) revises the main research projects undertaken in the Anglo-Saxon countries that have contributed to the unquestionable improvement of the OPACs, among which we must mention: the Dewey Decimal Classification (DDC) Online Project, developed by OCLC in 1984–5; the OKAPI Project, started in the middle of the 1980s by the British Library; the Bibliographic Elements and Displays Project, from the University of Toronto, set in motion in 1994; and the Contextual Resource Evaluation Environment (CREE) Project, initiated in 2003 with the participation, among other institutions, of the universities of Hull, Oxford, Edinburgh and York, focused on the analysis and preferences of users for the use of different search tools and in various contexts.

For the user, the information display plays a crucial role when assessing the quality of a system interface and decisively influences the success of the information retrieval in it. Online catalogues have considerably increased the information scenario that they provide, and their design depends to a great extent on the MARC structure of the bibliographical records. There are a lot of people who consider that we are not taking full advantage of the potentialities of the current display systems and all this has moved the discussion to the cataloguing field.

A good number of recent works, Calhoun (2006), Marcum (2006), Mann (2006) or Markey (2007), suggest that the detailed attention paid to the descriptive cataloguing cannot be justified any longer, prevailing opinions in which the simplification of cataloguing is proposed, considering the possibility of removing the subject headings in favour of automatically generated metadata.

Another line of strong debate has been made clear in the Research Information Network report (2009: 37), where it is shown that the current processes of bibliographical records are imperfect and ineffective, having a bearing on the decrease of the value and usefulness for the end user of the individual libraries' catalogues and defending a redefinition of the standards and the quality of the records which let us consider the availability of shared catalogues. The RIN study emphasises the need to develop business models in which libraries, publishers, aggregators and content distributors or companies such as Google, among other, work together.

The OCLC projects on the use of metadata, culminating in the integration of CORC (Cooperative Online Resources Catalogue) in the WorldCat, have to be combined with the main proprietary companies of library management systems that have made it possible for the OPACs to offer any type of documents, whether in MARC or in Dublin Core. In this context we should add the discussions arising at the heart of Web 2.0 that are aimed at social OPACs. An example such as LibraryThing[12] (Figure 4.2) illustrates new ways of information display and a way of grouping the bibliographical references undoubtedly close to that proposed in the FRBR model.

Figure 4.2 LibraryThing

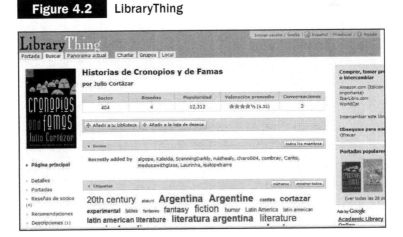

It was in 1991 in the IFLA Conference in Moscow that the Study Group on the Functional Requirements for Bibliographical Records (FRBR) was created. In 1997 in the Conference held in Copenhagen the final report was accepted and it was published in 1998 as Functional Requirements for Bibliographic Records: Final Report (FRBR). Since 2003 it is the FRBR Review Group that takes charge of promoting the FRBR model and issuing guidelines for its implementation in the creation of bibliographical and authority records, as well as encouraging its use in libraries, archives, museums, software industries, etc.

Despite all this, its implementation does not rise above the merely superficial, in spite of opinions such as those of Zumer and Riesthuis (2002: 80), who describe as revolutionary the structural framework of the FRBR model. In their opinion the OPAC is no longer considered as a sequence of bibliographical records, ordered according to strict rules or as a mere replica of the traditional catalogue in index cards in a computer, in order to evolve towards a network of connected entities. We should not ignore the previous need of introducing adaptations in the different rules of national catalogues, of harmonising its relations with the metadata field, of steering the FRANAR (Functional Requirements and Numbering for Authority Records) project safely through, in which the entity-relation is applied to the records of Authority and accommodate the MARC format to the new proposals of FRBR.

Martín González and Ríos Hilario (2005) analyse various prototypes of catalogues in which the new conceptual FRBR is used – Austlit Gateway, Virtua, LibDB and RedLightGreen – concluding that the implementation of the model in the online catalogues constitutes a significant development because it allows better and more complete information retrieval and a more effective organisation of records. However, they add, their advantages have to be proven, and for that it is necessary that some of these projects reach the end of the experimental stage and are used daily.

The IFLA dealt with the display of the bibliographical information in the online catalogues for the first time in 1998 in their *Guidelines for OPAC Displays*, published as a second version in 2005, in which a more modern and updated attitude is observed:

- The guides are based on three principles: To meet as a priority the users' needs, to give the highest importance to the content and the arrangement of the records and to call for the tracking of the international standards on the content and the structure of the information.

- They consider how a record configured under the FRBR model has to be displayed and describe the importance of the bibliographical relations in the OPAC.

- They include the need that the catalogue allows the appropriate navigation and visualisation of the authority records, allows navigation of all the authority records of a particular item, to display subject heading records related to a given one, etc.

- They have a direct bearing on the content, emphasise the need for the catalogue to include in an appropriate way links to the information external to the catalogue: electronic journals, full text articles, other catalogues, pictures, tables of contents, community information, etc.

In the collection of the bibliographical information of the catalogue, undoubtedly the thematic information and, particularly, the problems of its retrieval have occupied a good part of the scientific literature about OPACs. As an example we have the study by Marcos Mora (2004), whose conclusions corroborate lacks inherited by the catalogues since the 1980s:

- They do not facilitate subject access to users who have not clearly defined their need for information, or those who have indeterminate knowledge about the system.

- They do not offer enough information to the user in order to determine the relevance of the documents obtained, or facilitate the reformulation of the query to improve the results.

Villén Rueda (2006) insists that the indexation systems and, therefore, the subject authority control is still a matter pending in most of the institutions and considers absolutely necessary:

- Implement subject authority files with an appropriate synthetic (interrelated) structure in databases and library catalogues.

- Incorporate qualitative improvements in the indexing systems used and in the indexes display.

We agree with Professor Villén Rueda on the aforementioned aspects and on the need to carry on incorporating improvements; however, we think that in a good number of OPACS, specifically in academic and research centres, you can detect the determination to visualise the authority indexes, show the subject inputs related to one given or the possibility of using thesauri, although the use of controlled vocabularies requires a cognitive effort on the part of the user that clearly moves away from the current search habits.

Enrichment of the bibliographical records

This is one of the repeated demands required for the improvement of the OPACs, as has been said before. Peis (2000) points out that the increase in the thematic information relative to the monographs in the catalogues began in the

1970s. The project for the thematic enrichment of bibliographical records, known as SAP (Subject Access Project), directed by Atherton tends to be considered as the starting point for others such as the SAP-Sweden or the Mercury project from the Carnegie Mellon University.

In 1992 in the Library of Congress the BEAT (Bibliographic Enrichment Advisory Team)[13] was created to research and undertake initiatives aimed at broadening the usefulness of the bibliographical records. Among the first actions, several projects focused on the enrichment of the bibliographical records were included, incorporating the tables of contents.

Peis (2000) himself noticed that one of the most important and urgent possibilities of improvement of the online catalogue was the inclusion of descriptive information, which could come from the table of contents. Pappas and Herendeen (2000) highlight three great advantages derived from the incorporation of this type of information into the catalogue:

1. Table of contents helps the users to determine the relevance of the titles with respect to their information needs.

2. The contents page improves enormously the effectiveness of the information retrieval.

3. They are used as a complement to the subject cataloguing.

Duchemin (2005) indicates as enrichment elements: cover, table of contents, back cover, abstract, author bibliography and even excerpts from the work. Recently Powell (2008) has shown in his work the integration in the OPAC of the University of Michigan of digitalised materials in its collaborative partnership with Google. For their part, Byrum and Williamson (2006) allude in their study to results in which it is confirmed that the level of use of the enriched records in the library is far higher than that of the current records; it has even been proved that the same record may increase its use by 45 per cent when it includes the table of contents.

It is worth mentioning the Catalog Enrichment Initiative,[14] an initiative conceived in 2004 with the aim of encouraging the coordinated creation of tables of contents data from older publications, a collaborative project directed by Robert Kieft – Haverford College – in which some institutions such as OCLC, RLG, Library of Congress, etc. take part. The recent report from OCLC (Cahoun et al., 2009) emphasises the first-order importance that users give to data enrichment. Users wish to reduce the difference between the description of the bibliographical record and the item itself. We agree that libraries need to work together to share the costs involved in catalogue data enrichment.

The positive influence of online libraries allows that users and the library community consider at this moment as a fundamental added value the incorporation of the elements indicated in the OPACs; moreover, the ILSs have the technological solutions that make it possible and that allow the incorporation of enriched items. At this moment the preferential forms for the record enrichment are the purchase of the contents from the usual ILS vendor of the centre and the use of APIs which act on publishing companies and/or service providers such as Google or Amazon.

Catalogues 2.0

Fortunately, the overwhelming power of Web 2.0 has entered the catalogues. Just years ago we suggested the need for improvement of ergonomic aspects and its adaptation to the users: the personalisation of the query/retrieval formats, the Selective Dissemination of Information, the user profiles, etc. (Rodríguez and Alvite, 2004), at this moment, a good number of our catalogues try to improve on the Web 1.0 stage, marked by a hierarchical system-user communication and merely transactional.

'OPAC 2.0' is the bibliographical catalogue in which technologies and attitudes from Web 2.0 are applied (Margaix Arnal, 2007a). This same author (2007b), bearing in mind works such as those of Calhoun (2006), Álvarez García (2005) or the University of California Libraries Report (2005), lists the main functions required in a social OPAC:

- Allow the users to introduce tags, rating and comments in the bibliographical records.

- Let the users select documents as favourites, organise them in folders and share these folders with other users.

- Include tools from social networks.

- Allow subscription to personalised RSS channels.

- Customise the search: limiting it to the books that the user has on loan, only those that he has marked as favourites, only in his tags, etc.

- Allow the arrangement of the search results according to the social information (frequency with which it has been selected as favourite, frequency of loans, rating assigned by the users, etc.).

- Display icons for the most borrowed books or those that belong to the basic bibliography in a chosen subject.

- Display the information introduced by the users: tags, comments and assessments, show number of times it has been selected as favourite, or has been lent, etc.

- Display other books that have been lent together with the one being displayed or other related titles, creating a system of recommendations.

- Allow navigation through tags and social networks (see who has selected that book as a favourite, see other favourite books of that user, etc.).

The advantages of this new OPAC will benefit the library itself (strengthening the catalogue as a retrieval tool, giving better use of the collective intelligence in the indexation, assistance in the collection planning, improvement in the institution positioning, etc.) and the user (arrangement of customised mechanisms, improvement in the search and navigation options, thematic retrieval in natural language, active participation in the creation of value added to the contents of the collection, etc.).

As we have mentioned, LibraryThing is undoubtedly the model of bibliographical service 2.0 converted to a referent, both for its contributions to the model of OPAC 2.0, and for its innovative character in the display of information. The implementation of the LibraryThing for Libraries tools in various libraries, the successful projects such as the Penn Taggs tool from the University of Pennsylvania, applications 2.0 from freeware such as OpenBib[15] or Drupal,[16] are combined with the proposals of the library software distribution companies such as Primo from Ex Libris or Encore from Innovative.

The qualitative leap derived from the implementation of the functionalities of 2.0 is unquestionable; however, it is advisable to remain cautious, as in interpretations such as those of Roser Lozano (2008) who reflects on the library 2.0 to draw attention to the true background of innovations of this social Web. According to Lozano, we get the opportunity of transforming the library model radically, beyond the fact of adding technological innovations that are no more than a simple make-up.

Catalogues and the semantic web

The objective of the semantic web is that the web turns from being a collection of documents to become a knowledge base. Therefore, it is to be expected that the search according to concepts of the semantic web will replace the search according to comparison of character strings in the current web or syntactic web. In this context, it is evident that the libraries and their catalogues are in a privileged position to be included in that new web – Web 3.0. This consideration is backed up by the commitment to standards, the authority control, and the use of terminological control instruments. However, as Bennett (2007) points out, in general the OPACs don't take advantage of the expressiveness of the information they contain and still cling to interfaces based on static structures of predefined hierarchical navigation.

Yee (2009), using relevant projects from the FRBR Review Group, Library of Congress or DCMI/RDA Task Group[17] has created a model of RDF data adapted to the FRBR rules, raising doubts about the adaptability of RDF to the most sophisticated model of FRBR. For his part, Malmsten (2008) has described the tools and techniques used to transfer the Swedish Union Catalogue (LIBRIS) to the semantic web, being based on the use of SPARQL and following the line of work of the DCMI/RDA Task Group.

Likewise, some prototypes have appeared such as that described in the study by Papadakis et al. (2008), in which a tool based in AJAX is presented to navigate through the subject headings of the OPAC by means of a dynamic and interactive structure based on graphs. The core of this semantic application is based on the use of an ontology which covers the subject headings and their interrelations. The results of the implementation of this tool in the OPAC proved to help the user in the topic information retrieval, meeting the information needs in a quicker, more effective and more intuitive way. For their part, Felip Vidal and Orduña-Malea (2008) propose the NextLib prototype, made up of LibX – an extension of the FireFox browser – a semantic database, software for automatic data detection and an example-based learning programme. The integration of these four tools would provide a more interactive, efficient and user-oriented system, displaying also an emerging line of work in the research in order to improve the information retrieval in the OPACs.

Online catalogues for twentieth century users

Thanks to the web and the continued technological developments, the last decade has allowed the OPACs to present radical changes, huge collections of integrated information resources and indisputable improvements in their interfaces. However, the current context of information access and retrieval, dominated by intuitive interfaces and powerful search engines, represents an undeniable challenge for the libraries and their catalogues, a challenge which requires adapting the systems design to the real behaviour of the users.

Among the trends that can be noticed in the recent evolution of the OPACs, undoubtedly the most radical and productive is that derived from the incorporation of technologies and services to Web 2.0. It is urgent to exploit the functionalities of the social technologies, make the most of the opportunity that we are given with the users' active participation in the information system, the social enrichment of the records or the re-utilisation of contents. It is necessary for the library to involve users in the creation and development of content in order to show the potentiality and richness of the catalogues and grow together with the user.

Moreover, we emphasise the changes in the conception of the ILSs, the commitment to interoperability, the integration of different applications independent from the system – which share and re-use data (mashups) – and the appearance of competitive open source products which make it possible to implement more advanced OPACs. Interfaces tend to be simplified and to include increasingly advanced functionalities: algorithms of results arrangement according to relevance, faceted navigation, fuzzy technology, search suggestions, customised spaces, federated search, export results to bibliography managers, etc.

Even so, we must demand and promote continual innovations and adaptations: FRBR implementation, faceted navigation, the use of clusters, intelligent stemming and support of synonyms tables, the introduction of weight algorithms, use of feedback on relevance, a more exhaustive enrichment of records, multilingual search, improvements in the inadequate retrieval of information according to subjects including semantic applications, in which, apart from the classification and subject headings we should incorporate social information supplied by the users, information on the tables of contents, on possible citation analyses, etc.

We think that in the academic and professional context, quantitative and qualitative research projects are to be fostered, projects which let us suggest possible changes in the OPAC functionalities and not only in the interfaces appearance. It is necessary to know the use habits, the search strategies that have been adopted, preferences in the records presentation, the potential conceptual problems of the users, the understanding or not of the catalogue structure and of its capacities. Furthermore, monitoring the users' actions in the system will help us to determine strong and weak points in the descriptive cataloguing, in the authority control systems and vocabulary used, as well as to detect possible gaps in the development of collections. It is necessary to adapt and stress the users' training, which must go from the use of buttons to be focused on making them understand the structure and objective of a catalogue; it is required to study the real adaptation of automatic corrections or helps. In the same way we must assess the 2.0 services, measure the participation and re-use of the information, work in the users 'profiles' and in the identification modes.

In short, we need continued analysis and discussion, which involves also the software developers, in order to study how we wish to have our catalogues, whether or not we must integrate the OPACs in the web engines, how to incorporate the catalogues to projects immersed in the semantic web, and finally, how to keep a strategic view of the future and a relevant role in provision of information.

Information and reference services

Traditional reference services

The information and reference service is a key part of a university library, as it is charged with meeting users' information needs. Until quite recently, the information desk and reference collection were the only resources libraries used to answer patrons' inquiries, but nowadays there are many more tools, which we shall discuss below. In this first section, we shall make an in-depth examination of traditional reference services, which are still very important in university libraries, although today they are backed by other more modern and innovative techniques which make the service more effective.

Merlo Vega (2009) lists several objectives that any reference service must meet:

- It is an essential service, so patrons must be aware of it and use it. For this to happen, librarians must publicise the service and offer training on how to deal with the reference works and other information resources. It is important for the library to have suitable spaces set up for this kind of activity and to develop a simple system for receiving inquiries.

- All inquiries must be resolved satisfactorily, and this involves having a solid reference collection. It is also necessary to develop document access systems when the information required is not in the collection itself. It is a good idea to set up fruitful partnerships with the interlibrary loan service, as it will largely support this initiative.

The most common classification of the different types of inquiries or requests that reach the reference service is:

- *General information inquiries*. This includes questions on the organisation and structure of the library, timetables, lending procedures, consultations of electronic resources, layout of the collection on the shelves, etc.

- *Easy-to-answer inquiries*. As the name indicates, this kind of question tends to be closed-ended, that is, in the majority of cases they can be answered with a single word or even a yes or no. These inquiries can be on a variety of topics. Librarians usually have to check with reference and information sources and resources to answer this kind of inquiry.

- *Bibliographic information inquiries*. This category includes all the other questions, that is, the ones that require more elaborate information. The end product of this inquiry is a set of bibliographic references on a given topic or topics which will help the patron carry out a project or study.

With regard to the person in charge of a reference service, in addition to being an expert in searching for and finding information sources and resources, they must also have the right attitude, as this heavily influences the quality of the service, bearing in mind that patrons are the cornerstone of the library. There is a series of techniques that helps reference librarians to perform their jobs optimally, including:

- A smile, the most effective communication instrument.

- Calling the other person by name, which helps the professional's capacity to understand and engages both parties more.

- Practising active listening. To do this, it is a good idea to eliminate physical barriers, such as counters, and come out from behind them if necessary. Other techniques include not disconnecting from the patron, even though the librarian sometimes has to handle more than one matter at once; trying to keep eye contact, as when the relationship with the patron is reduced to a brief exchange of books, such as in loan transactions, the communication does not tend to be very fluid; observing body language, as the patron's gestures and postures will communicate many things; and finally, listening empathetically, putting yourself in the other's shoes. By following these guidelines, the communication between the two parties will be much easier.

When we defined the objectives that a reference service must fulfil in a university library, we mentioned the importance of a specific collection to respond to the inquiries submitted by patrons. Nowadays, we can talk about the printed reference collection, which exists in any university information service, but what are gaining more and more importance are specialised information resources available on the web. Many of them charge fees, so libraries have to pay a subscription; however, many others are free and open. In the early 1990s, Guinchat and Menou (1992) developed a classification of what we traditionally call a reference collection. They distinguish between three kinds of consultation or reference works:

- Bibliographies, catalogues and indexes, which refer to documents already analysed. They are used to respond to requests about works on a given topic, or by a given author, or to bibliographic inquiries.

- Dictionaries and encyclopaedias, defined as works that refer to ideas. This means that they will be useful for very specific, practical information requests. These works are the most appropriate for resolving occasional or easy-to-answer inquiries.

- Directories, guides and yearbooks, which contain specific addresses and information.

These authors classify other reference works into frequently consulted compilations of texts and figures like legal compendia and statistics; works that gain the value of continuity and integrity as part of a series, like reports, memos, norms, patents, etc.; and finally, discursive works that can serve as references, such as manuals.

With regard to information sources and resources on the Internet, Maldonado Martínez and Rodríguez Yunta (2006) present a list of highly useful tools that should always be a part of any reference service:

1. *Subject directories and indexes*. These organise electronic information resources into thematic classifications. They consist of hypertext lists of categories with subdivisions that hierarchically depend on the next higher level. The majority of these indexes also have a form for sending in direct inquiries. There are international, academic,[18] specialised and other sorts of directories.

2. *Search engines*. These are tools whose databases store a vast number of websites located by robots whose mission is to jump from page to page using hyperlinks. Each stored page is assigned a series of terms representing its content, which will serve as the access point for the searches conducted by users. Nowadays, the best search engine is Google[19] and all the other services it offers, including Google Scholar, Google Images, etc.

3. *Library websites*. Even though at first this kind of information seems like it is only useful for the library staff, actually these websites contain a great deal of information and links to resources chosen for their quality that are appropriate for all kinds of users, as shown in Figure 4.3, including library catalogues, online periodicals, official gazettes, e-journals, etc.

4. *Bibliographic databases*. This includes sets of information organised into registers and stored on an electronic support that can be read by a computer. A register consists of an autonomous information unit that is in turn organised into different fields or kinds of data. Usually this kind of resource is created and maintained continuously with the goal of resolving specific information needs. There are several kinds of databases, but the ones used most often in library reference services are document databases, which may include only the referential information that describes and locates the documents that it contains, or the complete text of these documents. As mentioned above, databases tend to be fee-based resources, meaning that the library must pay a fee every year to subscribe to them, although there are also free databases. Libraries tend to organise these information sources by thematic areas in order to facilitate users' access to them.

5. *Scientific e-journals.* These are collections of articles resulting from research activities that are published under a common title via the web, with a certain frequency and a stable content structure. They come from a variety of sources, as some e-journals were founded directly on the web, while others had previously been published on paper and were then adapted to the electronic medium. The contents are variable, although the journals usually offer summaries of each issue with the complete text of the articles, the latter usually for a fee. This kind of information resource is being constantly developed, and they are often upgraded. For example, some of the most common added-value services in e-journals are alerts that enable users to receive occasional information on the release of new issues through email; information searches related to the journal; searches for articles within the publication itself through summaries, author and subject indexes; guides to specialised resources in the journal's subject matter; discussion forums; access to supplementary material or appendices; inquiries as to evaluations of the articles by experts; downloads of bibliographic references and the ability to browse them; inquiry into the quotes from the articles; and RSS feeds that enable users to receive the contents of the journal as they are produced.

6. *Electronic reference works.* These are information and reference sources that can be used via the Internet, oftentimes free of charge and otherwise for a fee. The advantage of electronic dictionaries, encyclopaedias, glossaries, thesauruses, etc. is that they are easy to use, offer multiple forms of access to the information they contain, are constantly updated and are interactive with users.

7. *Internet media.* This includes online newspapers, news agencies, magazines, radio and television stations. These

resources have characteristics inherent to the web including interactivity, the immediacy and possibility for the news to be constantly updated, the multimedia or multiformat nature in which audio, video, texts and images coexist, functionality and personalised services.

8. *Open access resources.* According to Suber (2004),

> the literature on open access is digital, online, free of charge and exempt from the majority of copyrights and licence restrictions. What makes this possible is the Internet and the author's or copyright holder's consent. In most fields of knowledge, specialised journals do not pay the authors, who consequently may authorise open access without this affecting their incomes. Open access is fully compatible with peer review, and the majority of prominent open access initiatives in the realm of academic literature stress the importance of this point [...].

The two ways to reach open access are the green road, or self-archiving by the authors into archives, repositories or

---

Figure 4.3 Leon (Spain), University Library Website

open access repositories, and the gold road, or publication in open access journals. In this way, both institutional and subject-based repositories and open access journals are two other information resources or sources that should be carefully borne in mind in a reference service.

Virtual reference services

Virtual reference, digital reference or electronic reference is a 'reference service initiated electronically often in real-time, where patrons employ computers or other Internet technology to communicate with reference staff, without being physically present' (ALA, 2004; Wasik, 2000). Virtual reference has existed for more than a decade as a support for and complement to the information desk at university libraries. Even though their degree of implementation is not uniform in all libraries, there are more and more virtual services. Instant messaging and chatting are just some of the tools that are being introduced in library reference services, which we shall discuss in further detail below.

Wasik (2000) proposes a structured six-step process to implement any successful virtual reference service:

1. Informing, where preliminary research into areas of expertise and existing service areas is conducted.

2. Planning, where procedures, methods and policies that reflect the overall organisational goals are developed.

3. Training, including developing a training plan to prepare staff for the service.

4. Prototyping, where the service is tested and modified before launch.

5. Contributing, which involves publicity and resource development for service support.

6. Evaluating, which includes regular service evaluation to identify improvement opportunities.

Of all of these aspects that must be taken into account when offering a virtual reference service, the three most important are the staff team, marketing and assessment.

The team

In the opinion of Breznay and Haas (2003), it is crucial to have a team that is qualified to offer a high-quality service. Furthermore, it is also important to have three different positions within the group:

- Manager/Coordinator that will be the cheerleader, scheduler, troubleshooter and salesperson.
- Technical support, someone who has technical skills and can help set up the services.
- Web support, another important team member because this person will place the links in the proper places and will design the web pages and icons to make the project visible and successful.

Kovacs (2007) discusses the different skills and competences that the members of this team should have. She stresses three groups: technical skills, related to computer applications, software, equipment, etc.; communication skills, which are important for the dialogue with patrons to be as fluid as possible; and reference skills, which are coupled with knowing how to search for and locate information and manage information resources and sources. All the librarians on the working team providing services in the virtual reference unit must receive training in line with the job they must perform in order to later offer it to the users of the service. Bearing in mind the study by Gronemyer and Deitering (2009: 433) about librarians' attitudes to instructions in the virtual reference environment, 'it is easy to let the technology be a barrier to teaching and learning, but searching via virtual reference does not depend on new technology, it depends on policies, reference interview skills, and perhaps most important, attitudes that are geared towards looking for opportunities to put the patron in control of his or her learning'.

Marketing

This is a crucial activity in any university library, so we have set aside an entire section for it. Promoting and advertising the products and services offered within an information unit will help these units work smoothly. Barber and Wallace (2002) developed a list of ten tips for marketing virtual reference services (VRS), as follows:

1. *Treat your online services like a branch library.* Support them with appropriate budget and staffing for both developing and marketing 'the product'.

2. *Have a communications plan.* This plan should complement and extend your library's overall marketing plan. The look, tone and voice should be consistent with the image of your library. Assign a coordinator to manage and carry out the plan.

3. *Don't forget your most important audience.* The most important audience when launching any new service is staff. All frontline staff need to be up to speed, know the URL and be able to answer questions. They should understand both the message and why it's important for the library.

4. *Remember you're only new once.* The launch of a VRS is newsworthy because it is new and unique to libraries. Be sure to take advantage of it. Get out those news releases. Call those radio and TV stations!

5. *Focus on what's unique.* Online reference and other virtual services provide an opportunity to focus on what people say they like best about libraries – the expert, personalised service that librarians provide.

6. *Have a clear and consistent message.* One that you use over and over again in all publicity materials, e.g., 'Get answers in your pyjamas. Send your questions to ...' Make sure your 'salesforce' (the whole staff, Board, Friends, etc.) understands the message and is prepared to answer questions. Remember, simpler is better.

7. *Harness the power of word-of-mouth marketing.* Prepare and encourage all frontline staff to put in a plug for VRS at every opportunity. 'Have you tried our new *Ask a Librarian* service? Let me give you one of these bookmarks with the URL'. Ask ten satisfied customers to tell ten friends. Also encourage friends and trustees to spread the word.

8. *Track positive feedback.* Provide an interactive form for VRS customers to give feedback. Collect testimonials to use in your next wave of publicity. (Use names only with permission.) Remind your 'salesforce' to forward any positive comments they hear to the publicity coordinator.

9. *Work the web.* Seek links with other websites of schools, government and other organisations to bookmark or link from their homepage. Offer an e-mail newsletter to keep customers informed of developments.

10. *Evaluate.* Evaluation is critical to any marketing effort. Provide an interactive form for VRS customers to give feedback. Collect testimonials to use in your next wave of publicity. Track your publicity. Watch to see what works and what doesn't. Aim to do it better next time.

Assessment

MacClure et al. (2002) analyse the different indicators to bear in mind when assessing virtual reference services:

- *Number of inquiries received.* They recommend that you tally the inquiries received on an individual basis, in case there are several within the same message, and on a daily basis.

- *Number of responses given.* This indicator is closely tied to the first one and helps to analyse possible technology glitches and the effectiveness of the virtual reference interview.

- *Number of questions asked virtually but not fully answered by digital media*, which sheds light on the proportion in which this service is used, and is useful for staff planning and training.

- *Total reference activity.* This means the total number of inquiries received, without discriminating between those that were and were not answered.

- *Percentage of questions received through the virtual service compared to the total number*, an indicator that might be very useful for justifying the service.

- *Correct answer rate.* In order to tally this, we recommended that a peer-based review group or observer be appointed to analyse a set of answers individually.

- *Time elapsed between the question and the answer.* This indicator will show the efficacy and efficiency of the service.

- *Number of questions asked that received no answer*, including those only partially answered and unmet requests.

- *Kinds of questions received.* The categories that these authors propose include bibliographic, instructional, literature-related, quick reference, research, technical, outside the scope and others.

- *Number of forwards or number of times the user has been forwarded to another service within the library.* This measure will serve to support balanced collection development and to plan the scope of the service.

- *Saturation rate*, which is used to find out the degree to which the library's potential users are involved in the service.

- *Resources used per question.* This identifies the number of sources and resources used to answer the information requests. This indicator provides exhaustive information on the kinds of sources checked and their characteristics.

- *Return rate.* The goal here is to find out how many users come back to the service more than once. This measurement indicates users' degree of satisfaction with the service, although the data gathering and analysis to develop this indicator is tricky.

- *Number of digital reference sessions.* This includes visits to the service through the available applications: FAQ, chat, interactive digital video, etc.

- *Use of the service.* The main purpose of this indicator is to properly organise work schedules for the entire staff.

- *Technology used by the users.* This is primarily to adapt the library software and website to the virtual reference service, even though it must be standard so that it is compatible with all browsers.

- *Existence of the service.* It is important to determine whether the entire population is aware of the service provided. To ensure that they are, marketing campaigns must be conducted and data gathering procedures must be used which will help to evaluate the effects of this promotion.

- *Accessibility.* This includes factors like the time span when the service is available, the design of the website, compliance with web standards, ease of use, etc. In order to get this kind of information, librarians must hand out questionnaires, surveys or any other instrument for gathering data.

- *Expectations.* This indicator is recommendable when the virtual reference service is limited and the person in charge needs to know what aspects of it are in demand and which require more coverage.

- *Other sources* used to meet the demand, as before reaching the virtual reference service the user might have used other resources that they thought might help them answer their inquiry.

- *Reasons why the service is or is not used.* These indicators measure the success or failure of the service.

- *Improvements and additional services.* This includes the areas that are liable to being changed and improved based on users' suggestions.

- *Satisfaction of the staff working in the service.* The team working in the service has a great deal to say, so their opinions will help to improve the service.

- *Cost of the service* in relation to the overall library budget. This measurement is useful for drawing up the budget and allocating resources to the service.

Virtual reference service tools

As mentioned at the start, the virtual reference service is a complement to face-to-face service. Both pursue shared goals, but the means of achieving these goals or the way that they are communicated to users to respond to their inquiries and requests is different. While in the traditional reference system we spoke about the librarian's positive attitude and presence with the patron and willingness to answer any question, in the virtual service these considerations will be important, but not as important since the patrons are no longer in front of us, rather we use other means of communication and transmission to respond to their inquiries. *E-mail* and *web-based forms* are the two easiest alternatives in a virtual reference service, which is why both are being implemented at all university libraries. E-mail is users' favourite method, as they can send in their inquiries from home without having to go to the library. Even if the library has not yet formally created a virtual reference desk, users can always resort to e-mail to get in touch with a librarian and make any kind of inquiry. Likewise, web-based forms are a more elaborate system than e-mail, yet they provide the library with the possibility of beginning the reference interview with the user in a passive way. This kind of form is created using empty boxes or fields to be filled in by the users, and they tend to be linked to the library's FAQ system.[20] The recipient of the forms is the reference service, whose librarians will be in charge of answering and resolving all questions and inquiries sent in.

Chat and instant messaging (IM) are other tools used in virtual reference services at university libraries. Their implementation in information units is not as widespread as e-mail and web-based forms, but many libraries now respond to information requests from users in real time and synchronically, as both the sender and the receiver are present at the same time. Both applications work in the same way, but using different technologies.[21] The heads of information services that use these tools as a means of communicating with their users usually set up a timetable, although in libraries with highly developed virtual reference units this service is open the same hours as the library. In order for communication between the librarian and user to be possible, specific programmes like X-*Chat, ChatZilla, m*IRC, AOL *Instant Messenger* or *Meebo* must be used. As shown in Figure 4.4, the reference service at Amsterdam University Library[22] uses instant messaging.

| **Figure 4.4** | Chat in Virtual Reference Service, Library of the University of Amsterdam |

In addition to offering chats as a means of communicating with its users, Amsterdam University Library also offers telephone and e-mail as a way of sending in inquiries in a timetable from 9:30 am to 5:00 pm.

It is still rare to see *IP telephone* and *SMS* (Short Message Service) being applied in reference units. However, there are two other means through which librarians can answer users' inquiries. Telephone conversations via the Internet are possible thanks to free programmes like Skype and Google Talk. In the case of short messages, in the majority of cases users must pay for the messages they receive. Since January 2010, Fairfield University Library[23] has been offering a new mobile messaging service for sending in any question to a librarian.

We do not want to close this section without talking about the *programmes* that have been specifically designed for performing a wide range of jobs within a virtual reference service. One of the most widely used applications at university libraries is QuestionPoint,[24] developed by OCLC and the Library of Congress. It is a cooperative online reference service with an up-to-date database on the questions and answers that users send in, which libraries hiring the service may access. It offers a complete reference management system, integrating chat, e-mail, and chat widget (Qwidget), live help 24/7 through membership in the 24/7 Reference Cooperative and work with colleagues locally or globally with cooperative staffing and referral networks.

Marketing services

Marketing in academic libraries: concepts and definitions

Marketing is the management process which identifies, anticipates and supplies customer requirements efficiently and profitably. (The Chartered Institute of Marketing)

Marketing is about collecting information, forecasting trends, consulting all concerned, understanding markets, formulating objectives, planning strategy, implementing strategies, evaluating everything and communicating with everybody. (de Sáez, 2004)

Good marketing helps libraries ensure their customers know the full range of services they have on offer, and that those services are being used to their full potential. (Toby Bainton, Secretary of SCONUL, 2008)

Marketing is the process of planning and executing the conception, pricing, promotion, and distribution of ideas, goods, and services to create exchanges that satisfy individual and organizational goals. (Glossary of Marketing Definitions, IFLA Section on Management and Marketing, 1998)

These are just four of the many definitions that have been given to the concept of marketing. Promoting products and services is a necessary practice in any organisation. Although marketing has long been associated with private enterprise, nowadays it has become a core activity in all kinds of organisations, including in the public administration. Leaders of university libraries are aware of the importance of using marketing techniques and strategies to make their service more effective and to boost the library's clientele, meaning that there is a wealth of marketing experiences and initiatives at university information centres. Likewise, we can detect an increasingly positive attitude among librarians towards marketing and their greater involvement in developing and promoting new services (Parker et al., 2007). Throughout this section, we shall analyse some of the concepts related to library marketing and then propose several practical suggestions.

Components of marketing

According to Shuter (1989), a marketing approach is made up of 14 elements:

1. *Consumers* or people who use the kind of product which the library provides.
2. *Customers* or people who exchange value for a library product. Apart from people using the library on their own account and people who obtain library products for others, in the public sector it is necessary to consider the many potential customers who are not consumers.
3. *Need*. This often refers to what librarians and community leaders *think* the community wants.
4. *Demand*. In contrast to *need*, demand is what members of the community are actually willing to use.
5. *Market segmentation*. This identifies the different

individuals in the community and groups them in relation to their need or demand for a particular product.

6. *Target markets.* In practice, the library is there to serve the whole community but, given that the market can be segmented in terms of likely demand, it is wise to identify target markets, or areas of likely demand to which the library can legitimately offer a product. Priorities can then be assigned to particular markets.

7. *Product.* This is a good or service which is exchanged for value with a customer and it is a complex concept in the public sector. So with libraries, the product is not the book or the book loan but what the loan represents to the user: an evening's entertainment, perhaps; help towards a qualification; help in putting up a shelf or cooking a dinner; increased understanding; greater profits, etc.

8. *Price.* The price is a combination of things: not merely the cost per ratepayer or the direct charge for a service like audiovisual materials or reservations. Librarians must consider the other costs to the user: money costs like fares; indirect costs like time and inconvenience involved in a library visit or the personal costs.

9. *Packaging.* In library terms, this is the system which wraps up the product. It is closely linked to price and is possibly its major component. One example of packaging is the classification system, supposedly designed to make information easily available. Libraries which package effectively base their services on the empowerment of the individual rather than the technicalities of traditional librarianship.

10. *Place* is the location where the product is available. It includes availability of products for home use, provision of reading or study space in the library, location of special collections, etc.

11. *Promotion* in two senses: *image promotion*, where an organisation is seeking a favourable public attitude, and *product promotion*, where the organisation is trying to gain customers.

12. *Decision marketing.* This means to decide what the library should be doing and uses decision criteria such as resource availability and urgency to decide what it can do.

13. *Performance measures.* Each objective must include a means of measuring its accomplishment.

14. *Evaluation.* This must be a continuous process from the moment a decision is implemented, and the results of the evaluation may well contain lessons for future planning.

Marketing plan

This is a crucial step in marketing success for the academic library. It is a strategic document that will identify market position, status, objectives, and outline how they will be archived, resources required and results expected (de Sáez, 2004). According to de Sáez, the marketing plan should be framed as an operational objective within the library's strategic plan. As mentioned in the previous chapters, the library must sketch out achievable objectives and a clear line of action. Both are materialised in a strategic document that is crucial for the entire organisation and serves as a roadmap for all the professionals working in the library. Other important factors to bear in mind for a marketing plan in an information service to be effective include: staff training in marketing through workshops, market research, focus groups, etc.; gaining acceptance from the entire university community; audience; the marketing plan should run through the different stages and staff involved as it is developed; and timescales, as unexpected changes can always arise, which means that the plan must be flexible.

Likewise, a comprehensive marketing plan must include some of the elements analysed below:

- *Brief executive summary*: This describes the place of the academic library within the overall organisation and includes the plan's objectives and content.

- The relevant elements of the *mission statement*.

- *Environmental analysis*: This is conducted through PEST variables[25] or by examining all sorts of different external influences: political, economic, social, technological and legal.

- *SWOT analysis*[26] or a study of the strengths, weaknesses, opportunities and threats in order to reveal the status of the library at any given time.

- *Portfolio analysis*: This may be that a service could well be made available to other market segments, thus developing new markets.

- Specific, clear and realistic *objectives* of the marketing plan.

- *Market segmentation* or interest groups, which in a library will include everyone in the university community: professors, researchers, students and administrative professionals who use the service.

- *Marketing and market research strategies*, which we shall discuss below.

- *Marketing mixes recommended*

- *Evaluation methods*: They should be formative and the plan should be flexible enough to accommodate change, if needed, at evaluation stages.

- *The timetable*

- *Budget*

Marketing tips

In 2008, Akers published 40 Marketing Tips for Academic Libraries on a Shoestring Budget on her blog 'Marketing Your Library'.[27] This information is extremely useful for libraries lacking budgets earmarked exclusively for developing marketing programmes. Below are some of the tricks and tips that can help librarians to successfully launch their products and services without the need to spend too much money.

- Use both traditional print methods and electronic methods to promote services and resources.
- Strive to position the library's URL in highly visible locations.
- Don't limit your graphic identity to books.
- Solicit feedback on your website via surveys or comments and acknowledge them upon receipt.
- Create an online newsletter available from your home page.
- Work with the editor at the student newspaper to place a bulleted list of short, promotional blurbs about services, collections, resources, activities on an ongoing basis.
- Buy plastic countertop holders for promotional material.
- Review headings on your website to make sure the content is 'packaged' logically and is easily navigable.
- Invite students from design or public relations or marketing classes to critique your print material and messages.
- Consistently use the library's logo, URL and/or slogan on print material and electronic promotions.
- Use inexpensive items with your URL printed on them (pens, magnets, mouse pads, etc.) to promote your resources.
- Create friendly discussion and hang-out spaces; create interesting exhibits and displays which are up a month or so.

- Use campus bulletin boards to promote library resources.

- Place a news corner for library news on your website. Regularly add new photos and news.

- Promote services and collections by designing colour posters which can be printed on a large-format plotter and inexpensively framed and placed on easels.

Marketing in practice in academic libraries

Marketing cultures

Marketing is a practice that is now common in public services, despite the fact that the concept originated in and was inherited from private enterprise. However, it is not yet regarded as a priority in university libraries, and its degree of implementation differs from one library to the next. According to a study conducted by Singh (2009) on the marketing culture in 33 university and special libraries in Finland, very few libraries find marketing challenging and demanding and use modern marketing theories and applications for providing a successful customer-centred service. As a result, in the majority of them, marketing has not become very important, despite the fact that a strong market-oriented approach brings customers more satisfaction. Singh posits three kinds of marketing cultures in university libraries (see Figure 4.5):

- *The high flyers*: Strongly market-oriented libraries whose main focus is to identify and ascertain its users/patrons' information needs; thus, they try to put the customer at the heart of their activities. These are ambitious, innovative libraries that focus on using modern marketing tools.

- *The brisk runners*: Medium market-oriented libraries that put the most concerted effort towards goals which are

Figure 4.5 Marketing cultures in libraries (Singh, 2009)

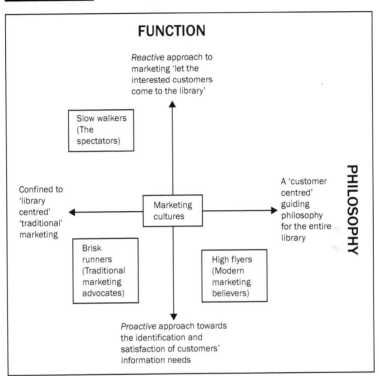

satisfied with traditional marketing approaches. Since they do not feel the need to come up with new methods, they use conventional marketing techniques.

- *The slow walkers*: Weak market-oriented libraries that have low profiles in market orientation, marketing attitudes, knowledge, operational activities and service performance. These libraries perform tasks oriented at promoting their products and services, but they are reluctant to call it 'marketing' and prefer instead to call it 'disseminating information'. Furthermore, the professionals working in this kind of library are called 'spectators', as they have a totally passive attitude towards these tasks.

Although it might seem somewhat counterintuitive at first, the marketing culture at university libraries in less developed countries has been quite advanced for more than a decade. Just to cite a few examples, Ghanaian academic librarians have been involved in implementing marketing strategies in their libraries, as they consider it important for achieving goals like retaining users, attracting others who have stopped using the library and securing financing (Martey, 2000). University libraries in Kenya use marketing techniques like public relations and advertising campaigns to promote a better perception of the library's role within the university, and in this way, just as in Ghana, they justify the aid they receive from different institutions (Kavulya, 2004). In turn, Kaur and Rani (2008) base the attitude found in professionals working in university libraries in India on the marketing practices of their libraries, which in theory is highly active and positive, although in practice they are not very sure about the strategies needed to put it into practice.

Marketing strategies

Throughout this section, we have spoken about several marketing strategies that are appropriate in libraries. Below is a list of the ones proposed by Alire (2007), Helinsky (2008) and Baltes and Leibing (2008):

- Sending *targeted e-mail alerts* to all the members of the university community and thus to library patrons. In theory, this seems like an efficient strategy, but information saturation from e-mail means that oftentimes communication between professionals and clients is less than fluid.

- Organising *training courses* so that all library staff can become familiar with the marketing techniques and tools that they can use to promote their service.

- Using the *institution's website* as a means of disseminating and promoting all the library's products and services.

- Taking advantage of the library's *intranet* as a means of communication and advertising.

- Using the library's *furniture* as a marketing tool by hanging materials at the strategically best spot along with the signs and guides needed to use them, etc.

- Using *media and publishing* to design marketing campaigns.

- Presenting *papers at congresses or workshops* on the library's efforts in order to share new experiences and initiatives. It is important to raise librarians' awareness that all day-to-day work has to be visible to the outside, as this is unquestionably the major marketing action that a library can do.

- Preparing *exhibitions, activities, games and competitions,* thus giving the library a role other than just a place to study and research.

- Making use of ICTs and *Web 2.0* tools to promote products and services: social and open software, mobile information devices, collaboration tools, mashups, etc.

- *Word-of-mouth* marketing which gets people to talk to others about library services.

- '*Guerrilla marketing*':[28] this is one alternative worth considering when the library only has a limited marketing budget.

Marketing experiences

As mentioned at the start of this section, marketing has become a real need in all information services. Specifically, university libraries must be innovative[29] with services and products that they offer, meaning that the director of the service must choose creative, versatile, proactive, empathetic people with sound communication skills to run their advertising projects. In some cases, librarians are reluctant to collaborate on promotion, advertising and marketing, as resistance of change triggers rejection of this kind of activity. For this reason, the leader should have the capacity and skills to know how to motivate their people, as just like in other kinds of projects, it is important for all the staff working in the library to get involved to some extent.

Below we shall share several particularly significant marketing experiences and initiatives conducted by university libraries that might serve as a pattern for others who would like to embark on a project of this kind.

Looking for the perfect slogan!

In 1999, the Rod Library at the University of Northern Iowa created a library marketing committee with the goal of heightening administrator, faculty and student awareness of library resources and services. Neuhaus and Snowden (2003) explain how for two years this unit was charged with promoting the library through newsletters, student surveys, advertising on pencil holders, t-shirts, etc. The library was aided in these efforts by library student assistants with artistic talents who drew pre-approved library slogans as sidewalk chalk art on prominent sidewalks around campus, such as:

> The end is near! – The library is here
>
> Looking for answers in all the wrong places? Try the library!
>
> Write on @ The Rod Library
>
> Get a clue @ The Rod Library
>
> Knowledge is power. Information is power. Power up at the Rod Library
>
> Way too busy – feeling down? Too much homework

makes your frown? We turn those frowns – upside down! @ The Rod Library

Brewerton (2003) shows how 'inspiration ... available now from the library' was the slogan used by the Oxford Brookes University Library[30] at Freshers' Fair 2000. The Inspiration Campaign used striking images like Newton's apple, Rodin's *The Thinker*, a penny dropping and a light bulb plus this slogan to promote the library's website (see Figure 4.6).

The library silk screened these designs on t-shirts, posters, stickers and other materials and used them to promote the

Figure 4.6　Images from The Inspiration Campaign

launch of its new website. The number of visits to the site rose as the campaign's effects were felt.

In turn, the American Library Association keeps a list of slogans that can help many libraries to create advertising campaigns on their products and services. The list is quite extensive,[31] but a few examples include:

The Ultimate Search Engine @ your library

Volunteer @ your library

Untangle the Web @ your library

Food for thought @ your library

Everything you want to know about everything you want to know @ your library

Reward the best!

Prizes are a reward received by a person or institution for a job well done. In the case of libraries, if the prize is considered worthwhile, the professionals working in the service will be more motivated and will work more actively to earn it. Prizes are also a good marketing strategy for university libraries, as they bring prestige, recognition and, in most cases, money. In recent years, the Marketing Academic and Research Libraries Committee of the Association of College and Research Libraries (ACRL) was charged with organising the Best Practices in Marketing Academic and Research Libraries @ your library award. All the winning libraries were given a plaque and a monetary prize of $2,000. In 2005 the American University Library[32] and Illinois State University Library[33] won the prize, while in 2007 the Booth Library[34] and the Winston-Salem State University Library[35] were the winners. All these institutions demonstrated strategies and practices that can be adapted to other academic libraries to effectively market their resources and services to the campus community.

Likewise, since 2003 the IFLA has been organising the International Marketing Award in which all kinds of libraries take part. The goals of the prize are to reward the best library marketing project worldwide each year, encourage marketing in libraries and give libraries the opportunity to share marketing experiences. In the 2009 edition, first place was awarded to National Library Board (NLB)[36] of Singapore, and the slogan for the winning campaign is 'Go Library'. This marketing project is a multi-platform project which aims to entice customers to the library. Significant inroads were made in outreach efforts, e.g., to schools, institutes and organisations, where there is an increasing need to make the library relevant to those technologically inclined who may receive information from online search engines or other non-conventional mediums. The library received airfare, lodging and registration for the 2009 IFLA General Conference and Council[37] and a cash award of $1,000 to further the marketing efforts of the library.

Change your library's image!

Gambles and Schuster (2003) demonstrate in a study how in 2002 Birmingham Libraries launched a marketing campaign to change their image and introduce a new branding. According to these authors, the goals of the campaign were the following:

- Increase overall number of visitors to libraries.
- Increase number of Internet users.
- Increase numbers of book borrowers.
- Increase user numbers of family history service.
- Increase library use by under-represented ethnic minorities and socially excluded groups.
- Increase library use for learning and study.

The image change consisted of designing ten slightly

different messages that stressed the point that libraries are changing and that libraries offer products that are relevant to young lifestyles. Successful examples (see Figure 4.7) included:

> Mice don't bite in the library – learning centres to teach you new technology. Birmingham Libraries are changing – learn how.

> Cure your headache in the library – health information to keep you feeling good. Birmingham Libraries are changing – check it out.

> Try yoga in the library – workout with health and

Figure 4.7　One of the ten successful messages

fitness books and videos. Birmingham Libraries are changing – is it time you did?

Takeaways in the library – choose from over 250,000 recipes. Birmingham Libraries are changing – take away a book today.

Low-cost promotion

Cronin and O'Brien (2009) tell how the Waterford Institute of Technology Libraries[38] (Ireland) was able to adapt to the prevailing financial climate, to engage in cost-effective initiatives and to promote itself and its services successfully. In academic year 2007–8, WIT Libraries launched a series of low-cost marketing experiences whose main feature was the low cost of creating and disseminating them, give that the library used 2.0 tools to publicise them. Several of these initiatives included:

- *Fines Amnesty on Books (FAB)*: For two days, WIT Libraries waived all fines on all standard loan books returned, irrespective of overdue date. The campaign was advertised using traditional techniques including distributing fliers and posters and word of mouth. They also used web technologies including e-mail, blog posts, RSS and the library website as methods of advertisement.
- *'Q-ness' Quiet Study Campaign*, which instigated a strategy to promote a defined quiet study area for students. The WIT Libraries utilised branded fliers, posters and blog posts to advertise the campaign.
- *Staff publications and presentations*: WIT Libraries staff are proactively involved in writing articles for various scholarly journals, delivering presentations at seminars and national conferences and getting involved in national committees and strategic review groups.
- *Signage*: WIT Libraries removed all existing signage and

literally started again. This can have positive effects aesthetically, for patrons and for the physical environment within the library, and it is a chance to brand the library at an operational and strategic level.

- *Surveys*: WIT Libraries has carried out two library surveys in an attempt to gauge user satisfaction levels of library services and inform future service delivery.

Play and learn at the library!

We cannot close this section on library marketing without discussing another strategy used by librarians to publicise and disseminate their services. The idea is to introduce play into libraries as yet another element. Even though this seems somewhat unusual at first, many librarians are organising events related to different sorts of games in order to attract more users to their services. As examples, we can cite a game night and a tournament that have been held at Z. Smith Reynolds Library (ZSR)[39] of Wake Forest University since 2005; the gaming program at the Claremont Colleges Libraries,[40] which includes weekly game nights, periodic tournaments and videogame-related lectures, and the gaming station, Library Carnival or Murder Mystery Event organised by the Libraries of Fairmont State University.[41] These events offer the Library staff an opportunity to meet students and learn more about the culture of gaming, and even play a few games themselves.

Notes

1. *http://www.exlibrisgroup.com/*
2. *http://www.iii.com/*
3. *http://www.aquabrowser.com/*
4. *http://www.sirsidynix.com/*
5. *http://www.worldcat.org/*

6. *http://rebiun.crue.org/*
7. *http://www.amazon.com/*
8. *http://www.vtls.com/products/visualizer*
9. *http://www.koha.org/*
10. *http://drupal.org/project/drupal*
11. *http://www.extensiblecatalog.org/*
12. *http://www.librarything.es/*
13. *http://www.loc.gov/catdir/beat/*
14. *http://www.loc.gov/standards/catenrich/*
15. *http://openbib.org/*
16. *http://drupal.org/*
17. *http://dublincore.org/dcmirdataskgroup/*
18. One example of this kind of directory is INTUTE, which contains information organised by large areas of knowledge (*http://www.intute.ac.uk*).
19. *http://www.google.es*
20. This association is useful, as the librarian recommends that the user review the list of FAQs before sending in a question, given the fact that oftentimes the FAQs contain the solution to the problem.
21. According to Francoeur (2008) chat programmes offer co-browsing, page pushing and the ability to form multi-library staffing groups, and IM programmes are externally hosted services that have been adopted by more libraries as a result of their low learning curve and prevalence among college-age individuals.
22. *http://cf.uba.uva.nl/en*
23. *http://www.fairfield.edu/library/lib_refappointment.html*
24. *http://www.questionpoint.org/*
25. PEST analysis *http://www.quickmba.com/strategy/pest/*
26. SWOT analysis *http://www.quickmba.com/strategy/swot*
27. *http://www.marketingyourlibrary.com/*
28. The term 'guerrilla marketing' describes unconventional marketing campaigns and/or strategies which should have a significant promotional effect – this at a fraction of the budget that 'traditional' marketing campaigns would spend for the same goal (Patalas, 2006).
29. Innovation is the managed effort of an organisation to develop new products and services or new uses for existing products

and services. It can be *radical*, if there are new products, services or technologies that completely replace the existing items in the market; *technical* if there are changes to a product, service or technology than involves the way the item is produced; *managerial* if there are changes in the way which products and services are conceived, built and delivered to customers; *product* if there are changes in the physical characteristics of performance of existing products and services, or the creation of brand new services or *process* if there are changes in the way products or services are manufactured, created or distributed (Rossiter, 2008)

30. *http://www.brookes.ac.uk/library*
31. *http://www.ala.org/ala/issuesadvocacy/advocacy/publicawareness/campaign@yourlibrary/prtools/yourlibrary.cfm*
32. *http://www.library.american.edu*
33. *http://www.ilstu.edu*
34. *http://www.library.eiu.edu*
35. *http://oklibrary.wssu.edu/*
36. *http://www.nlb.gov.sg*
37. The winner is announced officially at the IFLA press conference.
38. *http://library.wit.ie*
39. *http://zsr.wfu.edu/*
40. *http://voxlibris.claremont.edu/*
41. *http://library.fairmontstate.edu/*

References

Akers, S. (2008) *40 Marketing Tips for Academic Libraries on a Shoestring Budget (Aren't We All!)*. Available from: *http://www.marketingyourlibrary.com/2008/05/40-marketing-tips-for-academic.html*.

ALA (2004) *Guidelines for Implementing and Maintaining Virtual Reference Services*. Available from: *http://www.ala.org/ala/mgrps/divs/rusa/resources/guidelines/virtrefguidelines.cfm*.

Alire, C.A. (2007) 'Word-of-mouth marketing: Abandoning the academic library ivory tower', *New Library World*, 108(11/12): 545–51.

Álvarez García, F.J. (2005) 'Informatización (II): Sistemas integrados de gestión bibliotecaria y tendencias en automatización', in L. Orera (ed.), *La biblioteca universitaria*. Madrid: Síntesis, pp. 105–47.

Baltes, G. and Leibing, I. (2008) 'Guerrilla marketing for information services?', *New Library World*, 109(1/2): 45–55.

Barber, P. and Wallace, L. (2002) *10 Tips for Marketing Virtual Reference Services (VRS)*. Available from: *http://www.ssdesign.com/librarypr/download/odds_and_ends/marketing_vps.pdf*.

Bennet, M.J. (2007) 'Opac design enhancements and their effects on circulation and resource sharing within the library consortium environment', *Information Technology and Libraries*, 26(1): 36–46. Available from: *http://www.ala.org/ala/mgrps/divs/lita/ital/262007/2601mar/bennett.pdf*.

Borgman, C.L. (1986) 'Why are online catalogs hard to use? Lessons learned from information retrieval studies', *Journal of the American Society for Information Science*, 37(6): 387–400.

Borgman, C.L. (1996) 'Why are online catalogs still hard to use?', *Journal of the American Society for Information Science*: 47(7): 493–503.

Breeding, M. (2008) 'Automation system marketplace 2008: Opportunity out of turmoil', *Library Journal*, 133(1). Available from: *http://www.libraryjournal.com/article/CA6542440.html*.

Brewerton, A. (2003) 'Inspired! Award-winning library marketing', *New Library World*, 104(1190/1191): 267–77.

Breznay, A.M. and Haas, L.M. (2003) 'A checklist for

starting and operating a digital reference desk', in B. Katz (ed.), *Digital Reference Services*. New York: The Haworth Information Press, pp. 101–12.

Byrum, J.D. and Williamson, D.W. (2006) 'Enriching traditional cataloging for improved access to information: Library of congress tables of contents projects', *Information Technology and Libraries*, 25(1): 4–11.

Calhoun, K. (2006) *The Changing Nature of the Catalog and its Integration with Other Discovery Tools: Final Report, Prepared for the Library of Congress, March 17.* Available from: *http://www.loc.gov/catdir/calhoun-report-final.pdf.*

Calhoun, K. et al. (2009) *Online Catalogs: What Users and Librarians Want. An OCLC Report.* Available from: *http://www.oclc.org/americalatina/es/reports/ onlinecatalogs/fullreport.pdf.*

CIBER (Centre for Information Behaviour and the Evaluation of Research) (2008) *Information Behaviour of the Researcher of the Future.* London: School of Library, Archive and Information Studies, University College London. Available from: *http://www.ucl.ac.uk/ infostudies/research/ciber/downloads/ggexecutive.pdf.*

Cronin, K. and O'Brien, T. (2009) 'Practical low-cost marketing measures: The experience of Waterford Institute of Technology Libraries', *New Library World*, 110(11/12): 550–60.

De Rosa, C. et al. (2006) *College Students' Perceptions of Libraries and Information Resources: A Report to the OCLC Membership.* Dublin, OH: OCLC. Available from: *http://www.oclc.org/reports/pdfs/studentsperceptions.pdf.*

de Sáez, E.E. (2004) *Marketing Concepts for Libraries and Information Services.* London: Facet.

Duchemin, P.-Y. (2005) 'L'enrichissement des catalogues? Et après?', *Bulletin des bibliothèques de France*, 50(4).

Available from: *http://bbf.enssib.fr/sdx/BBF/pdf/bbf-2005-4/bbf-2005-04-0021-004.pdf.*

Felip Vidal, L. and Orduña-Malea, E. (2008) 'NextLib: un sistema de programari basat en ontologies per a la consulta automàtica de l'OPAC des de llocs web especialitzats', *BiD: textos universitaris de biblioteconomia i documentació*, 20. Available from: *http://www2.ub.edu/bid/consulta_articulos. php?fichero=20felip1.htm.*

Francoeur, S. (2008) 'The IM cometh: The future of chat reference', in S.K. Steiner and M.L. Madden (eds), *The Desk and Beyond: Next Generation Reference Services*. Chicago: Association of College and Research Libraries, pp. 65–80.

Gambles, B. and Schuster, H. (2003) 'The changing image of Birmingham libraries: marketing strategy into action', *New Library World*, 108(1192): 361–71.

García López, G.L. (2007) *Los sistemas automatizados de acceso a la información bibliográfica: evaluación y tendencias en la era de Internet*. Salamanca Universidad de Salamanca.

Garza, A. (2009) 'Next generation OPACs: Part 2. From OPAC to CMS: Drupal as an extensible library platform', *Library Hi Tech*, 27(2): 252–67.

Gronemyer, K. and Deitering, A.-M. (2009) 'I don't think it's harder, just that it's different: Librarians' attitudes about instruction in the virtual reference environment', *Reference Service Review*, 37(4): 431–4.

Guinchat, C. and Menou, M. (1992) *Introducción general a las ciencias y técnicas de la información y documentación*, Madrid: CINDOC.

Helinsky, Z. (2008) *A Short-cut to Marketing the Library*. Oxford: Chandos.

IFLA Section on Management and Marketing (1998) *Glossary of Marketing Definitions*. Available from: *http://archive.ifla.org/VII/s34/pubs/glossary.htm.*

IFLA (Study Group on the Functional Requirements for Bibliographic Records) (1998) *Functional Requirements for Bibliographic Records*. Available from: *http://www. ifla.org/en/publications/functional-requirements-for-bibliographic-records*.

IFLA (2005) *Guidelines for Online Public Access Catalogue (OPAC) Displays: Final Report May 2005*, Saur, München.

JISC and SCONUL (2008) *Library Management Systems Study. An Evaluation and Horizon Scan of the Current Library Management Systems and Related Systems Landscape for UK Higher Education, Study Report*. Available from: *http://www.jisc.ac.uk/media/documents/ programmes/resourcediscovery/lmsstudy.pdf*.

Kaur, A. and Rani, S. (2008) 'Marketing of information services and products in university libraries of Punjab and Chandigarh (India): An attitudinal assessment of library professionals', *Library Management*, 29(6/7): 515–37.

Kavulya, J.M. (2004) 'Marketing of library services: A case study of selected university libraries in Kenya', *Library Management*, 25(3): 118–26.

Kovacs, D.K. (2007) *The Virtual Reference Handbook: Interview and Information Delivery Techniques for the Chat and E-mail Environments*. London: Facet.

Lozano, R. (2008) 'Biblioteca 2.0: Revolución o nuevo maquillaje para viejas formas de hacer?', *ThinkEpi*, 21 July. Available from: *http://www.thinkepi.net/biblioteca-20-%c2%bfrevolucion-o-nuevo-maquillaje-para-viejas-formas-de-hacer*.

MacClure, C.R. et al. (2002) *Statistics, Measures and Quality Standards for Assessing Digital Reference Library Services: Guidelines and Procedures*. Syracuse, NY: Syracuse University.

Maldonado Martínez, A. and Rodríguez Yunta, L. (ed.) (2006) *La información especializada en Internet: directorio de recursos de interés académico y professional.* Madrid: CSIC.

Malmsten, M. (2008) 'Making a Library Catalogue Part of the Semantic Web', *Proceedings of the International Conference on Dublin Core and Metadata Applications.* Available from: *http://dcpapers.dublincore.org/ojs/pubs/article/view/927/923.*

Mann, T. (2006) *The Changing Nature of the Catalog and its Integration with Other Discovery Tools. Final Report. Prepared for the Library of Congress. Critical Review.* April 3. Available from: *http://www.guild2910.org/AFSCMECalhounReviewREV.pdf.*

Marcos Mora, M.C. (2004) 'El acceso por materias en los catálogos en línea: análisis comparativo de interfaces', *Revista Española de Documentación Científica,* 27(1): 45–72.

Marcum, D.B. (2006) 'The future of cataloging', *Library Resources & Technical Services,* 50(1): 5–9.

Margaix Arnal, D. (2007a) 'El OPAC 2.0: las tecnologías de las Web 2.0 aplicadas a los catálogos bibliográficos', in *Actas del VI Workshop CALSI* Available from: *http://www.calsi.org/2007/wp-content/uploads/2007/11/didac_margaix.pdf.*

Margaix Arnal, D. (2007b) 'El OPAC Social, el catálogo en la Biblioteca 2.0. Aplicación y posibilidades en las bibliotecas universitarias', in *10as. Jornadas Españolas de Documentación.* Santiago de Compostela: Fesabid, pp. 199–203.

Markey, K. (2007) 'The online library catalog: Paradise lost and paradise regained?', *D-Lib Magazine,* 3(1–2). Available from: *http://www.dlib.org/dlib/january07/markey/01markey.html.*

Martey, A.K. (2000) 'Marketing products and services of academic libraries in Ghana', *Libri*, 50: 261–8.

Martín González, Y. and Ríos Hilario, A.B. (2005) 'Aplicación de los Requisitos funcionales de los registros bibliográficos (FRBR) en los catálogos en línea', *ACIMED*, 13(4). Available from: *http://bvs.sld.cu/revistas/aci/vol13_4_05/aci05405.htm*.

Merlo Vega, J.A. (2009) *Información y referencia en entornos digitales. Desarrollo de servicios bibliotecarios de consulta.* Murcia: Universidad de Murcia.

Neuhaus, C. and Snowden, K. (2003) 'Public relations for a university library: A marketing programme is born', *Library Management*, 24(4/5): 193–203.

Novotny, E. (2004) 'I don't think I click: A protocol analysis study of use of a library online catalog in the internet age', *College & Research Libraries*, 65(6): 525–37. Available from: *http://www.ala.org/ala/mgrps/divs/acrl/publications/crljournal/2004/nov/Novotny.pdf*.

Pace, A.K. (2004) 'Dismantling Integrated Library Systems', *Library Journal*, 19(2): 34–6.

Papadakis, I., Stefanidakis, M. and Tzali, A. (2008) 'Visualizing OPAC subject headings', *Library Hi Tech*, 25(1): 19–23.

Pappas, E. and Herendeen, A. (2000) 'Enhancing bibliographic records with tables of contents derived from OCR technologies at the American Museum of Natural History Library', *Cataloging and Classification Quaterly*, 23(4): 65–7.

Parker, R., Kaufman-Scarborough, C. and Parker, J.C. (2007) 'Libraries in transition to a marketing orientation: Are librarians' attitudes a barrier?', *International Journal of Nonprofit and Voluntary Sector Marketing*, 12: 320–37.

Patalas, T. (2006) *Guerrilla-Marketing-Ideen Schlagen Budget*. Berlin: Cornelsen.

Peis, E. (2000) 'Tablas de contenido de monografías con carácter colectivo y enriquecimiento de registros bibliográficos', *Boletín de la Asociación Andaluza de Bibliotecarios*, 15(59). Available from: *http://www.aab.es/Baab59a3.html*.

Powell, C.K. (2008) 'OPAC integration in the era of mass digitization: The MBooks experience', *Library Hi Tech*, 26(1): 24–32.

Research Information Network (2009) *Creating Catalogues: Bibliographic Records in a Networked World: A Research Information Network report*. Available from: *http://www.rin.ac.uk/our-work/using-and-accessing-information-resources/creating-catalogues-bibliographic-records-network*.

Rodríguez Bravo, B. and Alvite Díez, M.L. (2004) 'Propuesta metodológica de evaluación de interfaces de OPACs. INNOPAC versus UNICORN', *Revista Española de Documentación Científica*, 27(1): 30–44.

Rossiter, N. (2008) *Marketing the best deal in town: Your library. Where is your purple owl?*, Oxford: Chandos.

Rowley, J.E. (1998) *The Electronic Library*, 4th edn. London: Library Association.

Salse Rovira, M. (2005) 'Panorámica dels sistemes de gestió de biblioteques al segle XXI', *BiD: textos universitaris de Biblioteconomia i Documentació*, 15. Available from: *http://www2.ub.edu/bid/consulta_articulos.php?fichero=15salse.htm*.

SCONUL (2008) *Librarians Share Good Practice in Marketing*. Available from: *http://www.sconul.ac.uk/news/market_lib*.

Shuter, J. (1989) 'Marketing and libraries', *Library Management*, 10(6): 27–30.

Singh, R. (2009) 'Does your library have a marketing culture?

Implications for service providers', *Library Management*, 30(3): 117–37.

Suber, P. (2004) *Creating and Intellectual Commons Through Open Access*. Available from: *http://www.cincel. cl/documentos/OpenAccess/suberrev052804.pdf*.

Tardón, E. (2002) 'De los sistemas integrales de biblioteca a los sistemas integrales de información', in J.A. Magán Wals (coord.), *Temas de biblioteconomía universitaria y general*. Madrid: Editorial Complutense, pp. 249–71.

University of California Libraries (2005) *Rethinking How We Provide Bibliographic Services for the University of California: Final Report, December 2005*, Bibliographic Services Task Force. Available from: *http://libraries. universityofcalifornia.edu/sopag/BSTF/Final.pdf*.

Villén Rueda, L. (2006) 'Indización y recuperación por materias en los opacs de las bibliotecas españolas: dos décadas de evaluación?', *El Profesional de la Información*, 15(2): 87–98.

Wasik, J.M. (2000) *Building and Maintaining Digital Reference Services*. Available from: *http://www.ericdigests. org/1999–4/digital.htm*.

Yee, M.M. (2009) 'Can bibliographic data be put directly onto the semantic web?', *Information Technologies and Libraries*, 28(2): 55–80.

Zumer, M. (2007) 'Amazon: Competition or complement to OPACs', *Bid: Textos universitaris de Biblioteconomia i Documentació*, 19. Available from: *http://www2.ub.edu/ bid/consulta_articulos.php?fichero=19zumer2.htm*.

Zumer, M. and Riesthuis, G.J.A. (2002) 'Consequences of implementing FRBR: Are we ready to open Pandora's box?', *Knowledge Organization*, 29(2): 78–86.

5

User-centred libraries

Information literacy

What is information literacy?

The term information literacy (IL) appeared in studies published back in the 1990s within the world of libraries, but it did not start to be widely used until ten years later. Cuevas (2007: 25) defines the concept as 'education in a set of competencies and skills related to the access, to use and evaluation of information'. Information literacy is closely related to digital literacy and is a key element in the networked society, the knowledge society and the society of lifelong learning. In a document entitled *Towards Information Literacy Indicators* published by UNESCO, Catts and Lau (2008) suggest another definition of the term. They claim that information literacy 'is the capacity of people to recognise their information needs, locate and evaluate the quality of information, store and retrieve information, make effective and ethical use of information, and apply information to create and communicate knowledge'.

Marti et al. (2008) list the different objectives pursued by information literacy:

■ To develop the skills to construct and implement an institutional programme of constant updating of knowledge on how to use the information and communication technologies (ICTs) and on methodologies for accessing and managing information.

- To offer tools and methodologies which help us to grasp the process of turning tacit knowledge into explicit, functional knowledge.

- To develop the skills to apply new knowledge, taking into account the psychological impact of adopting the new information and communication technologies on people's day-to-day lives.

- To reinforce individual and institutional ICT competences, as well as methodologies for accessing information and managing knowledge and aiding organisational and life change within the Information Society.

- To acquire new working habits when faced with major changes: new kinds of documents, new ways of communicating and new settings for communication and education.

- To conserve and re-circulate the knowledge generated in new sources of information based on evidence and lessons learned.

- To apply knowledge with innovation in order to solve novel, emerging and/or unknown situations.

- To effectively and efficiently apply knowledge in a process of constant improvement of everyday activities.

- To acquire confidence and total mastery of the fundamental concepts for using technological and methodological resources.

- To acquire new working habits in which the capacity to analyse complex situations predominates; to identify, analyse and solve problems; to plan, organise and critically evaluate extraordinary work situations.

IL is taking shape as an evolution in library patron training, a service that university libraries have been offering since the 1970s whose goal was to show and teach users how to use all the information services and resources they made available. Today, training at libraries goes a step further in that it is necessary not only to educate patrons in the use of sources and other information resources but also to give them the competences and skills needed to learn how to locate, choose and evaluate all kinds of information they might need over the course of their lifetimes. The document published by the ACRL (Association of College & Research Libraries) in 2000 entitled *Information Literacy Competency Standards for Higher Education* suggests a series of competences, divided into five standards and 22 performance indicators, which outline the process by which faculty and librarians identify a student as information literate. The standards focus on the needs of students in higher education at all levels and list a range of outcomes for assessing student progress towards information literacy:

- *Standard One:* The information literate student determines the nature and extent of the information needed.

- *Performance indicators:*
  - The information literate student defines and articulates the need for information.
  - The information literate student identifies a variety of types and formats of potential sources for information.
  - The information literate student considers the costs and benefits of acquiring the needed information.
  - The information literate student revaluates the nature and extent of the information need.

- *Standard Two:* The information literate student accesses the needed information effectively and efficiently.

- *Performance indicators*:
  - The information literate student selects the most appropriate investigative methods or information retrieval systems for accessing the needed information.
  - The information literate student constructs and implements effectively designed search strategies.
  - The information literate student retrieves information online or in person using a variety of methods.
  - The information literate student refines the search strategy if necessary.
  - The information literate student extracts, records, and manages the information and its sources.
- *Standard Three*: The information literate student evaluates information and its sources critically and incorporates selected information into his or her knowledge base and value system.
- *Performance indicators*:
  - The information literate student summarises the main ideas to be extracted from the information gathered.
  - The information literate student articulates and applies initial criteria for evaluating both the information and its sources.
  - The information literate student synthesises main ideas to construct new concepts.
  - The information literate student compares new knowledge with prior knowledge to determine the value added, contradictions, or other unique characteristics of the information.
  - The information literate student determines whether the new knowledge has an impact on the individual's value system and takes steps to reconcile differences.

- The information literate student validates understanding and interpretation of the information through discourse with other individuals, subject-area experts and/or practitioners.

- The information literate student determines whether the initial query should be revised.

■ *Standard Four*: The information literate student, individually or as a member of a group, uses information effectively to accomplish a specific purpose.

■ *Performance indicators*:

- The information literate student applies new and prior information to the planning and creation of a particular product or performance.

- The information literate student revises the development process for the product or performance.

- The information literate student communicates the product or performance effectively to others.

■ *Standard Five*: The information literate student understands many of the economic, legal and social issues surrounding the use of information and accesses and uses information ethically and legally.

■ *Performance indicators*:

- The information literate student understands many of the ethical, legal and socioeconomic issues surrounding information and information technology.

- The information literate student follows laws, regulations, institutional policies and etiquette related to the access and use of information resources.

- The information literate student acknowledges the use of information sources in communicating the product or performance.

In turn, Bainton (2001) presents an information skills model which attempts to illustrate the relationships between the 'competent information user' at the base level and the much more advanced idea of information literacy. The 'pillars' show an iterative process whereby information users progress through competency to expertise by practising the skills (see Figure 5.1).

Many international bodies have taken an interest in information literacy in university libraries. Proof of this is documents like the Prague Declaration: Towards an Information Literate Society[1] (2003) and the Alexandria Proclamation on Information Literacy and Lifelong Learning[2] (2005), which stress the importance of libraries and information services as providers of the tools needed for citizens' information literacy. Likewise, International Federation of Library Associations and Institutions (IFLA) has an Information Literacy Section from 2002 that focuses on all aspects of information literacy, including user education, learning styles, the use of computers

Figure 5.1 Information skills model

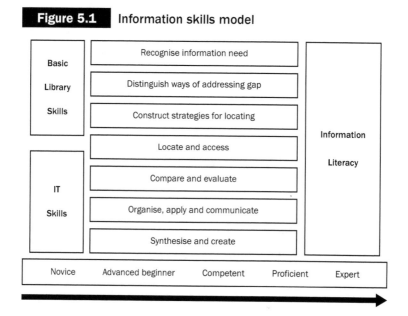

and media in teaching and learning, networked resources, partnerships with teaching faculty in the development of instructional programmes, distance education and the training of librarians in teaching information and technical skills. It has issued two documents to guide libraries and information centres: *Guidelines for Information Literacy Assessment*[3] dating from 2004, and *Guidelines on Information Literacy for Lifelong Learning*[4] dating from 2006.

The Information Literacy Coordinating Committee of the Association of College & Research Libraries (ACRL) has developed a variety of information literacy tools. One example is its website,[5] which is framed as a gateway to resources on information literacy helping users understand and apply the Information Literacy Competency Standards for Higher Education to enhance teaching, learning and research in the higher education community. Plus, it also offers a series of resources and ideas that facilitate library professionals' jobs, including a glossary of related terms, a standards toolkit, information on assessment issues and bibliographies.

Likewise, the main goal of the Society of College, National and University Libraries (SCONUL) and its Working Group on Information Literacy is to ensure that the role of information literacy in learning and teaching, research and organisational enhancement is communicated effectively and understood by the wider educational professional groups in higher education. In 1999, the Working Group drew up a baseline document entitled The Seven Pillars of Information Literacy,[6] which aims to define what was meant by 'information skills'; to articulate why information skills are important for higher education students; to assess the size and scope of current activity in higher education in the UK and Ireland and to identify principles of good practice in this area.

Projects worth noting in Spain include ALFIN-EEES,[7] a pilot initiative being coordinated by a professor from the

University of Granada, María Pinto. Its mission is to serve as proposed contents for the main generic competences related to information literacy, which are valid for any university student who needs to look for, manage, organise and evaluate information gathered from a wide variety of sources. Another worthwhile project is the Alfin Red forum,[8] a virtual community for studying, researching, promoting and implementing information literacy services.

Information literacy as a strategy in university libraries

Strategic planning and goal-based management are practices that have been in use at university libraries for many years. It is important for each institution to be aware of its priorities and to plan which jobs and services it must perform and what resources it has to perform them. Usually all of these predictions come together in a document called a strategic plan, which serves professionals as a procedure book for organising jobs within the service. Strategic plans at university libraries have a similar structure and tend to be organised into three parts:

1. Strategic strands, which correspond to the organisation's three main areas of action.

2. Strategic objectives, which outline the goals to be met within each of the overarching strands.

3. Operational objectives, which correspond to specific projects and help to ensure that the strategic objectives are fulfilled.

As mentioned above, information literacy has become one of the main missions of academic libraries, so much so that the majority of them include it within their strategic strands of action:

'Incorporate fundamental research skills and concepts into the first-year experience and general education and continue to build on these skills through the major to ensure that all graduates are competent in their ability to use information resources in their chosen career and are prepared for life-long learning' (Strategic Plan 2007–2012 of the Meriam Library, California State University, Chico).

'Improve the quality of student learning through improved teaching practices. Contribute to improved information literacy teaching practice within flexible learning environments to enhance graduate capabilities' (Library Strategic Plan 2009–2012 of La Trobe University, Australia).

Other libraries have even drawn up specific information literacy plans, such as the 2005 Information Literacy Strategic Plan of Louisiana State University, which was revised in 2009. It cites the following objectives:

- Collaborate with other programmes on campus to facilitate Information Literacy.
- Coordinate information literacy programme efforts to develop some progression of skills in students over the course of their college careers.
- Continue and expand the employment of online tutorials, especially by using demonstrably effective technologies including those which promote interactivity.
- Determine student and faculty information literacy needs and the effectiveness of the overall Louisiana State University Library Instruction programme.

Information literacy programme design

If we want information literacy to play a prominent role in libraries, it must be included as a specific strand within the library's strategic plan. It is also wise to draw up a specific programme that includes all the aspects that must be reviewed before beginning training, as listed below:

1. *Mission, goals and objectives*, which include a definition of information literacy, reflect sound pedagogical practice, articulate its integration across the curriculum, accommodate student growth in skills and understanding throughout the college years, etc. (ACRL, 2003).

2. Drawing up a calendar that provides a detailed description of the *type*, *levels* and *models* of training that are going to be taught at the library and the *tools* that will be used. Information literacy programmes at university libraries are usually designed with both a face-to-face and a virtual component in mind. As we shall explain in other chapters, many universities are using e-learning platforms to teach their distance courses. Libraries are now taking advantage of these systems to launch virtual information literacy programmes, usually with the support of face-to-face teaching.

   The IFLA and ACRL distinguish between three models of information literacy:

   - Access to information, determining what information is needed and how to find it effectively and efficiently.

   - Critical evaluation of information to incorporate it into knowledge and values.

   - Use of information, using it ethically for a specific purpose and understanding the related economic, legal and social issues.

Training at university libraries is mainly targeted at all patrons that use the service, including: students at all levels (bachelor's, master's and doctoral programmes, exchange students, etc.), teaching and research staff (full professors, associate professors, adjunct professors, visiting professors, grant awardees, associates, etc.) and administrative and services staff (administrative assistants, scholars, economists and finance experts, IT workers, student support staff, university extension, etc.).

The tools libraries use to provide face-to-face training have not changed much over time: courses, guided tours, practice sessions, handbooks and presentations are the activities that predominate in the vast majority of programmes. However, virtual training requires another kind of resource that is compatible with e-learning platforms and makes learning easier. The 2.0 applications which we discuss in one of the sections of this chapters play an important role in distance learning. They include blogs, wikis, social networks, shared files, etc.

3. Seeking alliances and cooperation with other departments to facilitate the institutional recognition of this training is another factor to bear in mind within the information literacy programme. It is crucial to seek alliances at all echelons within the university: the academic organisation (chancellor, vice-chancellors, faculties and schools, departments and areas), the administrative organisation (management, human resources, etc.) and last but not least, students through the student delegates and representatives. Each group can support the inclusion of information literacy in their curricula and training programmes for the entire university community or the improvement of infrastructures for training, both face-to-face and virtual. Specifically, students have to be convinced that lifelong learning and training in the access to, evaluation and use of information is necessary for their studies; that what they learn at the university will later serve them to join an increasingly competitive job market. Even though this is an accepted reality, no matter how

much the library tries to raise their awareness, the power of persuasion truly lies in the teachers in their classrooms.

4. In turn, librarians must show a particularly positive attitude towards the new challenges facing them. Training is one function of the library that must be transformed into a patron service, meaning that information professionals must take on the role of teacher or trainer. Plus, a sound understanding of library resources adds value to them, so it is worth ensuring that all the staff working at the library gets involved in information literacy, each at his or her own level.

5. Assessment and evaluation of information literacy programmes, using performance indicators, is necessary in order to ascertain the positive or negative development of the process and detect errors that can be solved on later occasions. According to Lau (2006), there are different assessment methods to support students throughout the information literacy learning process. Here are the primary recommended tools (Figure 5.2):

- *Checklists*. These are lists to guide students in the accomplishment of their assignments and they include the different stages, levels or items necessary to complete the assignment. Checklists should be visual task reminders to improve student growth and should be provided at the beginning of the assignment so that they can be used during the whole learning project or task for self-feedback.

- *Rubrics* are a precisely structured assessment that guides students to achieve a successful performance. They normally include a graded list of the attributes students ought to perform in their learning tasks. The rubric can be divided according to the process steps with a clear indication of each element to be considered to reach the desired goal.

Figure 5.2 Assessment techniques

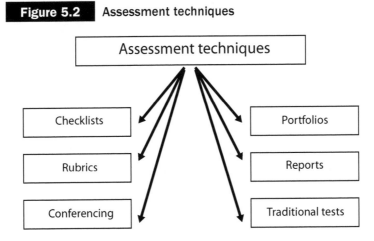

- *Conferencing* is a technique that is based on a discussion with the learner, among learners or among the whole class to orally reflect on the information literacy processes. It can be done at the different stages of the information tasks, as well as at the end of the process. It uses questions posed by the facilitator inquiring about the process of learning.

- *Portfolios* consist of accumulating student work over time and integrating it into a final package of IL process products. Portfolios are useful assessment techniques because they give students the chance to see their learning products become integrated into a final product. They are an excellent way to measure the efficiency of attaining the learning goals and evaluate the effectiveness of learning strategies and the clarity of knowledge presentation.

- *Reports* are useful essay exercises as long as they are not cut-and-paste exercises or a repetition of the information in printed or electronic sources with little synthesis or no evaluation of the retrieved information.

- *Traditional tests* or lists of questions with open-ended or structured answer options are also useful. Tests can be used when time is limited or when the assessment is specifically focused on a certain aspect of learning.

Proposed programme

In order for a university library to be successful in its mission to make its patrons information literate, it must properly plan its range of courses and other activities over the academic year. The alliances that have been reached with the different stakeholders within the institution will be utilised to ensure that the programme is fully included within the curricula. This is so that the library can provide ongoing compulsory training in all degree programmes as yet another class, and that the information literacy courses and activities are duly recognised and reach as many users as possible.[9]

It is also important to plan the information literacy programme by areas of knowledge. Students, faculty and administrative staff who are studying and working in similar fields usually have similar needs, so offering training targeted at general fields of knowledge is more effective.

Finally, we recommend that you organise the training for students by educational levels or years. Students who are in their first year of university often lack specific information knowledge, while those at higher levels usually have more advanced skills.

Below is a training proposal for a university library, along with the goals that it pursues:

Objectives

- To empower patrons to use the tools needed to ensure that they learn how to deal with, locate, select and disseminate information while taking advantage of its usefulness for other aspects of their life, both professional and personal.

- To develop skills and strategies for using the services and resources that the library offers and ensure that its patrons make better use of them.
- To learn how to use the university library and any other library autonomously.
- For the university library to encourage independent lifelong learning, making use of e-learning and self-study as well.
- To develop transversal initiatives and experiences with the support of other departments within the institution and targeted at different user groups.

Courses/Activities

- Guided tours of the library(ies)
- How to use the library catalogue
- Information management
- Information resources for researchers specialising in the different thematic areas
- How to conduct a research study
- Academic publication systems
- Copyright issues
- IT tools applied to teaching
- Open access initiatives
- Social web tools for students and researchers
- Academic journals with a wide impact
- Managers of bibliographic references
- Evaluation of research
- Study techniques
- 'Reserve a librarian'[10]

University repositories

The university in favour of open access

With the launch of arXiv[11] in 1991 by Paul Ginsparg, a new stage in the academic and research world opened. This is the first e-prints[12] repository on high energy physics, mathematics and computer sciences, created in Los Álamos Laboratory in the United States and which can be accessed freely through the Internet. This was followed by other open digital archives, such as RePEc[13] (Research Papers in Economics) and Cogprints[14] (Cognitive Sciences Eprints Archive), both of them created in 1997 with the same purpose as the first one: storing and managing digital contents, originated in the research, regarding two or more subject areas, in order that they may be consulted, openly, through the Internet. Twenty years later, we can talk about the total establishment of these services, so much so that the first positions of the Ranking Web of World Repositories (July 2009)[15] are occupied by subject digital deposits.

The EPrints[16] platform, developed by a team of researchers of the School of Electronics and Computer Science of the University of Southampton in 2000, is used to implement the first institutional repository, which in contrast to the subject one, includes research from a specific organisation. With the passing of time, new products have been developed for the creation of open digital archives and since the appearance of the first deposits organised by subjects, the proliferation of this type of services has been massive in universities and institutions targeted at the scholarly activity. Nowadays they have become one of the most innovative services in the academic libraries and almost compulsory in all the entities devoted to research.

The definition of institutional repository that is used most frequently is that contributed by Lynch in 2003:

a suite of services that an institution offers to its community for the management and dissemination of the digital contents generated by the members of that community. At its most basic level, it is an organizational commitment for the control of those digital materials, including its preservation, arrangement, access and distribution.

Steven Harnad contributes a literal meaning of the concept:

a place to deposit the digital contents of an institution. The main thing is to store the research results in order to maximize its use and impact.

And for his part, Peter Suber thinks that an institutional repository is

fundamentally the vehicle to reach the open access, it is more useful if it is interoperable, if it envisages the long-term preservation of its contents and is accompanied by an effective institutional policy. It is also a living entity and the academic image within the organization.[17]

It is worth highlighting two of the ideas suggested by Suber in this last definition. On one hand, the substantial competence that the author grants to the institutional repositories is combined with the idea of the Budapest Declaration in 2002, one of the bases of the open access movement in the world, which establishes two routes to reach this type of access: the golden road, which proposes publication in open journals and the green one, which refers to the deposit of digital materials in institutional or subject repositories (self-archive). And on the other hand, the fact that these services are backed up and supported by policies duly defined by the government team of the organisation that creates it must be a priority condition to be considered before their development. However, in most of the institutions, the supporting policies of Open Access have been emerging in parallel to the implementation of their repositories and do not overtake them.

The boost that universities have given to the repositories has been unequal. Some of the universities have established the mandate to self-archive all the research generated and subsidised by the entity itself in the institution repository. In theory, this first measure should be the most effective one as all the scientific information that was generated at the university would be quickly accessible to everybody through the Internet and in this way the increase of contents in the repositories and consequently their progress would be guaranteed. But not all the authors follow this trend and think in the same way. Whereas Harnad states the need for mandates in order to maximise the growth and to guarantee the success of the institutional repositories, McGovern affirms that other criteria favour their consolidation, including the use that may be made of their contents and the financial and technical support which they obtain. He also points out that the mandates may give rise to more problems than benefits (Harnad and McGovern, 2009).

ROARMAP[18] (Registry of Open Access Repository Material Archiving Policies) is a record that exists on a worldwide scale about self-archiving policies (see Figure 5.3). At present,[19] it includes 139 mandates and 15 proposals, most of them coming from universities and agencies that finance the research. Among the most relevant and recent mandates, we may cite the mandate of the North American National Institutes of Health[20] (NIH), in which, with the approval by the US Senate of the Act FY2008 'Labor, Health and Human Services and Education and Related Agencies Appropriations' the researchers who

Figure 5.3   ROARMAP

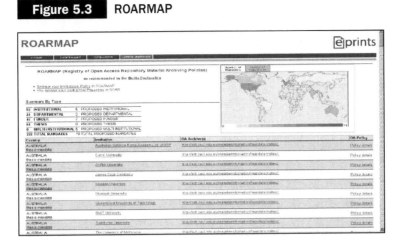

receive subsidies from them have a duty to deposit copies of their texts in PubMedCentral[21] before one year has elapsed since publication in a journal with peer review. These new regulations break away from their previous policy of voluntary deposit, approved in 2005 and in force until 2008.

In the University of Harvard,[22] the Faculty of Arts and Sciences and the School of Law are the institutions that initiated these types of mandates in 2008, specifying that the teachers who approve, by a large majority, these mandates have the obligation of depositing all their research in the institutional repository of the university. They are followed by the School of Education and the John F. Kennedy School, which also have adopted a self-archiving mandate and, finally, the School of Medicine, which has already registered its proposal.

The MIT (Massachusetts Institute of Technology)[23] launched its mandate in March 2009, with the unanimous approval of the teaching staff, which commits to send to a representative of the principal's office the final version of its works in electronic format and free of charge. That office will be in charge of placing this digital material in the institutional repository.

In Spain, the Regional Community of Madrid, in its role as financial agency, approved, in February 2009, the compulsory requirement according to which the research groups that receive financial aid for R&D programmes must self-archive a copy of their published works or the final version of them in the institutional repository available for this purpose in its university, public research agency and/or the repository independent from the Community of Madrid, within six months for the technology and bioscience areas and twelve months for social sciences and humanities, of the publication of those works.

The reaction of the authors to the mandate of their institution varies according to the source consulted. According to a study made by Swan and Brown (2005) of the views of the researchers on open access, 95 per cent of the teachers who were asked answered that they would have no objection to self-archiving their works in the repository of their university, if the institution required it. However, an earlier study, written by Rowlands et al. (2004) shows that 38 per cent of the interviewed authors would resist the order or mandate and would not accept compulsory self-archiving. Although the results of these surveys may be somewhat contradictory, they seem satisfactory, noting a positive change in attitude to the open access initiative on the part of the authors; in a short period of time, all the surveys coincide in the fact that the scientist has two viewpoints, that from the author and that from the reader and his/her attitude varies according to the fact that it fulfils one or other function. On one hand, the researchers/authors resist self-archiving their works due to the quantity of barriers that they find and on the other hand, the researchers/readers are in favour of self-archiving, because they wish the scientific communication process to be fluid.

As we have already discussed, all the university repositories obtain institutional support at a different level. Up to now we have talked about the mandate and about how many universities adopt this rather strict type of open access policy. But it is not always like this, other options exist, intermediate measures, less extreme, that foster and promote the existence of the repositories, their support and evolution and we group these below:

- *Text signature and declarations in favour of Open Access*: such as, for example, *Berlin Declaration on Open Access to Knowledge in the Sciences and Humanities*.[24] This is a document signed in October 2003, whose mission is 'support new possibilities of knowledge dissemination, not only through the classical manner, but also using the paradigm of open access by means of the Internet'. They define open access as 'a wide source of human knowledge and cultural heritage approved by the scholarly community. In order to achieve the view of a global and accessible knowledge representation, the web in the future has to be sustainable, interactive and transparent. The content and the software tools must be freely accessible and compatible'. In addition, they advise the researchers 'to deposit a copy of all their published articles in an open access repository and encourage them to publish these articles in open access journals'. So far[25] 266 institutions have signed the Declaration and, therefore, recommend open access as a scientific communication route.

  Another very recent example is *Compact for Open-Access Publishing Equity* (COPE)[26] from September 2009. The first signatories of this document were five North American universities: Cornell University, Dartmouth University, Harvard University, MIT and University of California at Berkeley, which recognise a 'crucial value of the services provided by scholarly publishers, the desirability of open access to the scholarly literature, and the need for a stable source of funding for publishers who choose to provide open access to their journals' contents' and commit to 'timely establishment of durable mechanisms for underwriting reasonable publication charges for articles written by its faculty and published in fee-based open-access journals and for which other institutions would not be expected to provide funds'.

- *Definition of repositories internal policies* includes four aspects: the use of data and metadata; their content and characteristics, as document typologies to be included and definitions; self-archive procedures, authorised access, embargos, etc; and, finally, the preservation and processes for the long-term conservation of materials. There are a few repositories registered in ROAR and in OpenDOAR[27] which have established this type of policy, but, to cite an example of good practice, that of the University of Nottingham[28] has defined perfectly all these aspects related to the internal operation of its service.

- *Economic funding on the part of the universities for the opening of results of scientific research.* Therefore, the University of California at Berkeley started in January 2008 a project called 'Berkeley Research Impact Initiative'[29] which tried to cover the publishing costs in open access of its authors. In this way, the teaching staff, post-doctorate and graduate students could request financial aid of up to $3,000 to cover the publishing costs of an article in open access, apart from covering the expenses (to $1,500) of 'hybrid publications', in which the information is accessible free of charge, but the journals limit the redistribution rights. The pilot programme was conceived to last 18 months or until the allocated funds of $125,000 run out. For their part, two other North American universities,

University of North Carolina-Chapel Hill and University of Wisconsin-Madison, following the trend of California, launched two analogous projects with objectives similar to the first one.[30]

- *The creation of specialised services*, from which assistance, guidance and support are offered to the teaching and research staff from each university, above all the aspects related to the open access: self-archive, copyrights, commercial publisher policies, etc. In June 2009, the team of SHERPA,[31] from the University of Nottingham, inaugurated its *Centre for Research Communication* (CRC), which houses the services, initiatives and projects in open access that currently are being implemented in that university, among which we can include the SHERPA Association, the RoMEO Open Access services, Juliet, OpenDOAR, the Repositories Support Project service and the contribution of the University to the DRIVER, Dart-Europe and NEOCBELAC projects. Bill Hubbard, who is responsible for the project, defines the objectives of the service: 'we aim to develop innovative research and development activities across the whole field of research communication. This is an exciting time for authors and researchers. We are beginning to leave behind straightforward electronic analogues of our centuries-old print world and realise the possibilities of new and far richer forms of scholarly communication'.

Therefore, despite the universities recommending self-archiving through all these measures, there are many barriers that are imposed on the authors in the process of depositing electronic copies of their works in the repositories of their institution. Most of them resist self-archiving their works simply due to ignorance and they are not aware of the advantages that it may contribute to their careers. Other people are frightened by the lack of control that may follow their articles being deposited (plagiarism, conflicts of interest, etc.). To these reasons we can add: lack of time, lack of familiarity with the information technologies, resistance to change, lack of motivation, objection to sharing results, etc.

Users of university repositories: principal stakeholders

Jones (2007) identifies different stakeholders for the university repositories and each of them will have different responsibilities and tasks within it. This author groups them in four categories which we list below:

1. *End users.* In the first instance, the members of the university community who use the library to meet their communication needs. *Teachers, researchers, students and other staff,* who work at the university, form this first group of stakeholders, although we can also talk about end users from other institutions, as the essence of any repository is that it is openly and, therefore, freely accessible to everyone through the Internet.

2. *Information providers.* Within this group, Jones draws together the authors, peer reviewers, publishers and libraries-information services. *Authors* are indispensable for the creation of the repository contents, as they produce and spread the results of their projects and researches. Within a university, they are the members of their community, that is to say, teachers, researchers, students and another administration staff the main recipients of this information, although as we have already mentioned, depending on the role adopted, they act as information providers or as end users.

   At the heart of scientific publications, *peer review* is a critical assessment that experts who are not part of the editorial team of the journal make of the manuscripts that reach them in order, among other things, that works of poor quality are not published, that the research results are correctly interpreted and that texts are selected in relation to the readers' interests (Hames, 2007). In general, the university repositories do not include this type of review, but most of them differentiate the works that have been subject to a peer review process from those that have not. The fact that the contents which are deposited in the university repositories are not being controlled by an experts committee, as in a scientific journal, is another of the problems that many researchers put forward in order to self-archive their research in them. As a proposal for the future, it would be appropriate to suggest some verification system within the university repositories, because nowadays this type of filter is necessary for the research assessment and for the consequent recognition of the scientific author.

Publishers are considered another important stakeholder in the scope of the university repositories. The functions that they fulfil in the traditional scholarly communication system is what Scovill (1995) has summarised in three sections: publish and produce, where we can include themes regarding the quality control of the publications (not only the content, but also the language or style), of the format or design of them and of the document treatment of the articles (indexation and abstract), legal and financial aspects, where we can include all the procedures related to the contracts with authors, management of the copyrights of articles already published, etc. and marketing through which all the products that the publisher markets will be released. But in the context of digital edition, the role of the publishers differs and, according to Jones (2007) would be to establish their position in relation to the type of content that they would like to see deposited in the open access digital archives. In addition, and according to the author, all these changes that have come up in the process of scientific communication are having a serious effect on the business of all the commercial publishers, although they have been responsible for much of this transformation.

Libraries and information centres are the last stakeholder which is an information provider. Several authors agree on the fact that the university libraries contribute actively to the evolution of the scientific communication and play an essential role in the establishment of institutional repositories. Their development has allowed the librarians to put into practice technological capacities and skills, unknown in the past by the users, so that their professional field gains greater relevance in the academic world. Librarians acquire and create electronic resources, while they make the content of them accessible more easily. They are experts in the areas of communication, preservation, metadata management, promotion and dissemination (Crow, 2002; Horwood et al., 2004; Read, 2008). Moreover, it is very common that in a university the library is the entity that is in charge of the directing and coordination of the institutional repository project, so that the librarians are those who adopt the role of manager of those repositories. But not all the authors think in the same way. According to Brown and Swan (2007), the repositories management is one of the seven more important roles which an information professional in an academic library plays, and 61 per cent of the researchers think that it will be an essential activity that the librarians will have to develop in the next five years. Or we could even take into account the opinion of Ottaviani, who considers that leading the repository projects in the universities is a responsibility of the librarians, as they show capacities and skills, not unique, but very adequate for a task like that (Ottaviani and Hank, 2009). However, there are opposite views, such as that of Hank, who maintains that the leadership must not be exclusive to the librarians and that they must share it, because it is necessary for the collaborative work with the other stakeholders in order to build up a good repository (Ottaviani and Hank, 2009). Hernández Pérez et al. (2007) are categorical when stating the benefits that are perceived at the academic libraries when these adopt a leadership role in the institutional repositories: greater recognition on the part of the research community because they can offer new and better services, such as reports about quotations and document downloads from the institution or supply of data necessary for the evaluation of the research community.

3. *Information mediators.* This third group is made up of other services which also are information suppliers, but in an indirect way, such as the aggregators and the academic search engines. The function of these information intermediaries is that of gathering data from the repositories, through only one interface, regardless of the computer program and the technical characteristics that each of them may offer.[32]

The aggregators[33] and the repositories are interoperable thanks to the Open Archives Initiative (OAI),[34] which should not be confused with the acronyms of the Open Access (OA). Taking into account the definition by Suber (2007), the OAI, initiated in 1999, defines a protocol, the OAI-PMH (Open Archives Initiative-Protocol for Metadata Harvesting), to collect metadata from data archives which are in separate archives. When the protocol is used by data services as search engines, these may process the data from separate archives as if they were in only one. In technical terms, the protocol for metadata collection supports the interoperability. In view of the good result obtained by the creation of institutional repositories and the exchange of information among scientists, the OAI has undertaken a new service called *OAI-ORE* (Open Archives Initiative-Object Reuse and Exchange)[35] (v. 1.0 17 October 2008), with the main objective of developing specifications that will allow the repositories to exchange web resources aggregations that set up information logical units (complex digital objects). Following the description that Rumsey and O'Steen (2008) give of OAI-ORE, it is a completely independent standard from OAI-PMH, and neither broadens it nor replaces it, but is focused mainly on the content, unlike OAI-PMH, whose objective is the metadata. According to this trend, it seems appropriate to highlight the project undertaken by the Texas Digital Library (TDL)[36] and its federated collection of electronic theses from the different public and private institutions that form it (see Figure 5.4). The experience consisted of adding support OAI-ORE to DSpace, a platform under which the collections of academic lectures are created. Once the results are obtained, the flexibility of the architecture of the computer program is under discussion and we can verify the benefits of adding extra functionalities of harvesting aimed at simplifying maintenance tasks of federated collections.

Jones also considers the academic search engines,[37] information mediators and as such, apart from recovering web pages, patents or monographs, they are able to gather every type of materials deposited in institutional repositories.

4. *Meta-information users.* Within this last type, the author draws together the *agencies* that finance *research,*

Figure 5.4 TDL repository

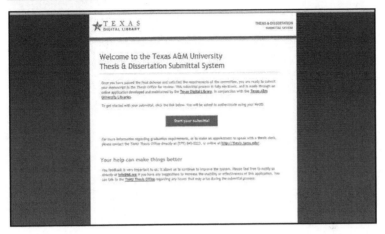

academic institutions and *national entities* that support with their policies the open access initiative and the existence of repositories. To cite but one example, the UK's Joint Information Steering Committee (JISC)[38] and SHERPA,[39] both British organisations, have been, from its beginning, very involved in the context of the digital repositories, through its projects, programmes[40] and events celebration.[41] In the Netherlands, SURF Foundation[42] stands out as an organisation that, in a way similar to JISC and SHERPA, works in a very active way in that subject.[43]

Academic libraries and repositories

As we have mentioned before, libraries and university information services are essential stakeholders of the institutional repositories. In most cases, it is from the library that the initiative of implementing the service comes, and the librarians are those who coordinate and lead the project and who ultimately have a great part of the responsibility, but it is very important to count on the help of other units and services of the institution. Analysing the SHERPA document, whose recent revision dates from March 2009 and in which the abilities and skills of the managers and institutional repositories are described, we notice that most qualities that are indicated in that document are typical of the librarians:

- Know the most relevant metadata standards: Dublin Core, MARC, METS, MODS, OAI-PMH, OAI-ORE.
- Identify and develop the metadata suitable for each case.
- Know how to define long-term preservation strategies.
- Have a good command of the description of the different existing document typologies and know their adequacy to the fact of depositing in a repository.

These aptitudes and others justify the importance that the librarian's work has within a project of institutional repository in a university and his/her experience and capacity make indispensable his/her presence in this type of initiatives from two points of view: on one hand, the internal tasks, related to the creation and implementation of the repository and, on the other hand, the external work, done with the aim of offering services that facilitate the use and management of this tool. With regards to the internal activities of the library and the librarians to set in motion an institutional repository, we can point out the following ones:

1. Creation of the list of *document types and formats* which can be included in the repository, as the librarians are experts in the management, description and analysis of the documents and know perfectly the characteristics of each. In the studies about the situation of the institutional repositories that have been prepared, generally according to countries or geographical areas,[44] the majority contents are doctoral theses and journal articles, but in a university

repository it is possible to include many others, such as: work documents, work submitted to congresses, scientific reports, teaching material, multimedia objects, datasets, etc.

2. Description and analysis of typologies included in the repository, in accordance with standards of suitable *metadata*. One of the tasks that a librarian has always carried out is the cataloguing of any type of bibliographical materials. The internal and external description of documents, in accordance with some established rules, has been a necessary task in order that the end users have at their disposal a catalogue which lets them identify and locate the documents in any library or information service. The same happens with the contents included in an institutional repository. The metadata generically defined as 'data about the data' are used to identify, describe and locate the digital objects included in it. The librarian will be the person in charge of choosing the appropriate standard, and in accordance with it he/she will analyse all the contents in the repository. At present the most used metadata model is the Dublin Core,[45] although most of the software platforms used for the creation of repositories admit other schemes, including PRISM,[46] MODS[47] and METS.[48]

3. Creation of a *list of subjects* or *vocabularies* for the thematic categorisation of the contents in the repository. The computer programs generally used tend to include a list of generic subjects, which do not correspond to the existing disciplines in each university. For this reason, the librarian must be responsible for the adaptation of the subjects to the contents and must customise the initial list, creating an individualised vocabulary for each institution. It is interesting to begin with a base glossary and to modify it progressively as new contents emerge and with the assistance of teachers, researchers and other authors.

Among the external work done by the libraries and the librarians to offer specific services that facilitate the use and management of the institutional repositories, we find the following tasks:

1. Suggest *marketing* strategies, in two senses essentially: on one hand, in order to extend the service to all the members of the institution and beyond it, and on the other hand, with the view to promote self-archiving on the part of the authors. In order to meet the first objective, the most effective method is to organise workshops where the service is presented and its benefits are discussed. It is advisable to devise a schedule and to structure the sessions according to interest groups: the university government team, deans and directors of schools, teachers, scholarship holders, students, administration and service staff, etc. In order to give incentives to self-archiving, there are different strategies, such as: general promotion, the development of services, the 'harvesting' of contents from other systems,[49] the review of the bibliographies of the researchers, the data about the use and the institutional policies (Mark and Shearer, 2006) or marketing done by the authors themselves who have already experienced the benefits of the documents deposit in a repository, such as, for example, the increase in citations (Zuccala et al., 2008).

2. Create tools for the *training* of all the university community in the use of the repository. The librarians will be responsible for drawing up the guides necessary for the service: on self-archiving, about copyright, on specific vocabulary, etc. In most cases, the library is the intermediary between the researchers and the service. All the doubts which could arise regarding it will be channelled to the library staff, so they must be prepared for every type of question, comment or suggestion.

Although all these tasks are in the hands of the library and its librarians, we cannot forget that every project in an institutional repository needs the assistance of other university services, such as that of the computing department, publications, legal consultancy, etc., so the institutional synergies and the cross collaboration would be aspects to take into account. If the relations among the different departments are good, then success is guaranteed and the repository will become a new vehicle to communicate the research, which will never replace the traditional methods, but will complement and improve them.

Digital collections

Digitisation in academic libraries

The earliest initiatives to digitalise[50] libraries and information services arose primarily to replace microforms,[51] which came to be widespread in American universities in around 1950. Within the library setting, this kind of material was used to store, preserve and conserve valuable documents which were difficult for patrons to consult. Nowadays, libraries all over the world have vast digital collections, and transforming printed matter to electronic contents has become a necessary process in any information unit. As a result, these services are receiving financial support from governments and companies in order to conduct massive document digitalisation projects which make it easier for patrons to access the collections via the Internet.

The benefits of digital documents are beyond question. Abby Smith (1999) suggests a few:

■ Their flexibility makes it easy to edit, manage, format and print an indefinite number of identical copies without the need for a paper copy. However, this quality also has its negative side, as the very plasticity of digital documents makes it easy for anyone to alter them if prior controls are not put into place.

- They facilitate access to information from anywhere on the planet, simultaneously by several users, with no regard for their coordinates in time and space.

- Unlike other formats like paper, photographic film or magnetic tape, digital formats do not deteriorate from being used or handled.

- Within the field of research, they provide access to certain teaching materials and special collections, such as rare books, manuscripts, images, etc., whose particular features make them unaffordable.

Hughes (2004), in turn, largely agrees with Smith and adds that the main advantage of digitalisation in a university library is that electronic documents foster access to all kinds of collections, to materials in all formats, and thus reach a wider audience. Furthermore, they help to preserve and protect the original documents, especially those with special physical qualities, and they contribute to collection development by merging or complementing the contents of other libraries. Hughes concludes by stating that digitalisation projects enhance an institution's strategic benefits by conferring more prestige on it, and that they also contribute to education and research within the scientific community.

University libraries have created special units made up of teams of expert professionals primarily occupied with planning and launching digital projects. Today, these departments have become the core of the information services, as they are in charge of implementing all library innovation programmes. As seen in Figure 5.5, the libraries

Figure 5.5 Stanford University libraries, digital collections and services

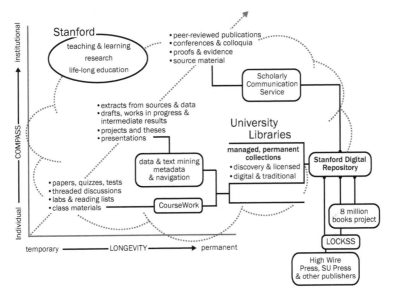

Source: SUL/AIR (2003)

at Stanford University have very clearly organised their digital services and collections. What stands out first is the prominence they are given in the teaching, learning, research and lifelong education of their patrons, and secondly the easy fit between the digital and traditional collections.

Each of these digital collections is targeted at different patron groups and meets different information needs. For example, peer-reviewed publications and proceedings from conferences and colloquia are fundamental documents for the research community, so in the Stanford model they are directly related to the Scholarly Communication Service, in addition to serving as essential components of the institutional repertoire. On the other hand, the users of teaching and classroom materials are mainly students in the many academic degree programmes.

153

The appearance and widespread use of digital services has enhanced the practice of traditional tasks at university libraries at times, and relegated it to secondary status at others, as they coexist without any conflict whatsoever. Despite the fact that there are recent studies showing a drop in interlibrary loans as a result of the surge in electronic information (Goodier and Dean, 2004; Echeverria and Barredo, 2005; Egan, 2005), following Willett (2009), the launch of massive digitalisation projects with limited availability on the web, which we shall discuss in the paragraphs below, will lead to a reinforcement of this traditional service, as the author claims that patrons will discover a larger number of sources that interest them yet are only partially available online. Likewise, Joint (2008) proves through statistics on use at English and American libraries that the circulation or loan of printed collections is rising every year and that many of the high-quality resources are only available on paper. Therefore, he concludes that this format should not be underestimated. However, it is a fact that at times of recession, institutions' limited monetary resources are channelled towards purchasing digital contents and restructuring the open spaces with technological facilities (Joint, 2009).

Digitisation policies, guidelines and plans

The European Union institutions have been charged with proposing the different policies on digitalisation for the member states. The most recent ones include:

- *i2010: Digital Libraries:* This dates from 2005 and addresses the need for digitalisation, online accessibility and the digital preservation of both the cultural heritage and scientific information. This initiative seeks to boost the efforts at encouraging European cooperation in this area, avoiding duplicated efforts, fostering the adoption of good practice and paying special attention to the efforts of national and repository libraries. All of this is expressed in specific programmes like *PRESTOSPACE*[52] (2004–2007), whose nine million euros in co-financing proposed a set of tools for digitalising audiovisual materials, and *eContentplus*[53] (2005–2008), which administered 60 million euros for projects aimed at improving the accessibility and use of European cultural and scientific contents with the goal of achieving interoperability among national digital collections and services.

- In 2006, the Council of the European Union encouraged the member states to address problems related to *digitalisation and online access to cultural material and digital conservation*, following a calendar that spanned from 2007 until 2009 and was based on the following actions: reinforcing national strategies and objectives on digitalisation and digital conservation, strengthening coordination among the member states, contributing to creating a European digital library, working together to provide a global vision of progress Europe-wide, and improving the framework conditions for digitalisation and the online accessibility of cultural material and digital conservation.

- Under the umbrella of the European Union's *7th Framework Programme*,[54] there are other projects underway related to the digitalisation of the cultural heritage and the coordination of libraries' efforts in this area: *DL.org* – Coordination Action on Digital Library Interoperability or Best Practices, and Modelling Foundations,[55] whose main objective is to 'create a framework where the leading representatives of digital library projects can work together, discuss experiences, exchange experiences, work on the interoperability of their solutions, promote shared norms and provide the community with new directions'; and PrestoPRIME,[56] whose mission is to develop strategies for the long-term preservation of digital objects and improve access to audiovisual collections. It also aims to develop a tool to convert metadata and a rights management system and record of digital fingerprints.

The United States has its own national digitalisation policies that help libraries take decisions on this issue. Worth mentioning are the 2007 'Draft Principles for Digitized Content'[57] from the Digitization Policy Task Force of ALA's Office for Information Technology Policy. This includes nine principles, each revolving around one aspect of digitalisation: digital libraries, digital materials, collaboration, sustainability, communication, international, education, preservation and standardisation. These country-based guidelines are joined by guidelines and handbooks of good practice for digitalisation projects which serve as institutions' baseline and guideposts when launching programmes of this kind.[58]

It is important for each library to draw up its own action handbook adapted to its own characteristics and needs, in that generally speaking prior planning of a digitalisation project in any organisation is necessary to ensure a satisfactory outcome. This general digitalisation plan will then lay the groundwork for the development of digital collections at a university library, will be a highly useful tool for all staff involved and will include all the factors to be borne in mind in a digitalisation project. Although we are not going to make an in-depth analysis of the entire process of format transformation, we do wish to stress four considerations regarding the pre-digitalisation phase.

Objectives, financing and preparation of collections

The tasks include setting realistic, achievable *objectives* while drafting a *monetary report* that includes all the expenditures the project will generate, as well as *choosing the documents* or collections to be digitalised. If the material resources are sufficient, the entire process is usually conducted inside the library itself. However, if the library does not have the appropriate technology, these tasks are then outsourced and a specialised company is charged with launching the project. If the library chooses the first option, it is important to forge alliances with other departments within the institution that can lend a hand and set up an action plan for each of the units involved. However, in both scenarios, the costs of digitalisation are quite high, meaning that some sort of financing must be allocated. Hughes (2004) lists five ways of securing financial support for projects, namely:

- institutional subscriptions;
- individual sales;
- outside grant support;
- institutional support from the host institution;
- revenue generation, for example by the provision of digitisation services.

The choice of material to be digitalised is the next step in the action plan. Figure 5.6 shows the range of collections a university library may have. In 2003 Dempsey and Childress of the OCLC Office of Research proposed this model, which shows the different types divided into four categories, each representing a different group of resources. The vertical axis represents the uniqueness of the content, while the horizontal axis shows the degree of conservation or stewardship the

Figure 5.6   OCLC collections grid

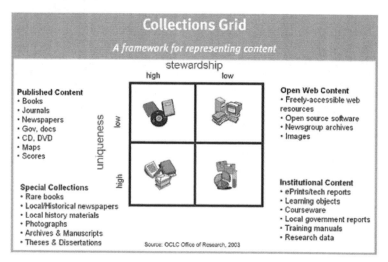

documents need. This grid may be highly useful when determining what kinds of documents should be digitalised.

Hazen et al. (1998) propose another strategy for choosing the most appropriate university library materials to digitalise. These authors pose a series of questions related to different aspects of the collections whose answers will guide the team in charge of the project as to whether to choose or discard the materials for digitalisation.

1. Related to the intellectual nature of the source materials, the intellectual quality of the collections must be assessed, including whether digitalisation will enhance their value, whether printed collections are sufficient for patrons and whether combining and relating them with other sources would raise their interest.

2. Related to current and potential users, it should be ascertained whether the collections to be digitalised are heavily used by patrons, whether their printed format or location hinder access to them and whether their physical conditions limit their use.

3. Related to actual and anticipated nature of use, it should be assessed whether the digitalisation of these collections will facilitate patrons' efforts and increase the use of the collections, whether researchers agree with digitalising them and whether the librarians and information experts are willing to help out in the project.

4. Related to the format and nature of the digital product, the material characteristics and physical qualities of the collections should be assessed and their resistance to change should be determined in order to ensure that they can withstand the transformation process.

5. Related to describing, delivering and retailing the digital product, the way to make patrons aware of the existence of digital collections should be determined, along with who will authorise access to these collections and under what circumstances, and finally, how the long-term preservation of these materials will be guaranteed.

6. Related to other digital efforts, inquiries should be made as to whether there already exists a digital copy of the materials and whether other departments within the institution will help to implement the project.

7. Finally, related to costs and benefits, the benefits to be provided by digital collections should be assessed, as well as whether the value of the intellectual content of the materials is proportional to the expense of the project, whether the digital collections will entail other long-term costs and whether there will be any external financing.

Copyright issues

Copyright is the next crucial point to bear in mind within the preparatory phase of a digitalisation project. All libraries must have a clear policy on protecting the copyright and intellectual property rights of the works in their digital collections. According to Prenafeta (2009), copyrights are the rights associated with original intellectual, artistic and scientific creations. Although it varies from country to country, we can generally distinguish between two kinds of copyrights. The first kind entails moral rights granted exclusively to the author (which are not transferable); they are protectionist and remain with the author throughout their entire lifetime and even after death (with certain conditions). The signatories[59] of the Berne Convention for the Protection of Literary and Artistic Works[60] do not all regulate moral rights in the same way. Continental law, which encompasses all the European countries except the United Kingdom, as well as much of Asia, Africa and Latin America, has legal systems that recognise moral rights. This tends to contrast with Anglo-Saxon law, which prevails in countries such as the United States, the United Kingdom, India and Australia; these countries usually do not recognise moral rights. One exception is the United States: even though in theory it does not admit moral rights, it does recognise these rights for visual artists in accordance with the 1990 *Visual Artists Rights Act*, with the proviso that these rights may be relinquished. The second kind entails proprietary rights, which are the ones that generate income, are transferable and have a limited timeframe which varies according to the laws of each country.[61] Proprietary rights include the exclusive rights (to reproduction, distribution and public communication) subjected to authorisation by the holder of the rights, along with rights to remuneration and compensation. Once these monetary rights have expired, the work comes into the public domain, meaning that it may be freely consulted without the need for any kind of restriction or permission.

As Labastida Juan and Iglesias Rebollo (2006) noted, with the arrival of the digital age, more flexible legal instruments are needed that enable works with acknowledged intellectual property to move more freely and be improved by people other than their creators. Hence the appearance of copyleft, which the same authors define, within this context, as an alternative to traditional or restrictive copyright characterised by the all-encompassing phrase 'all rights reserved'. Copyleft uses copyright to create a less restrictive system: any use of the works is allowed as long as the author is cited; when the original work is transformed into a new one, it is also distributed with the same licence. Today, the term copyleft is used to refer to all alternative licensing systems[62] as opposed to the traditional 'all rights reserved' model.

Bearing all this in mind, and pursuant to the *Handbook on Copyright and Related Issues for Libraries* put out by eIFL. net, before digitalising their collections, libraries must abide by the copyright laws in their countries, in addition to negotiating the terms and conditions of use of/access to the materials with the authors and publishers. Libraries must ensure that the contracts signed with the owners of the collections are the best for their patrons and are written specifically and clearly, and they must try to form consortia with other entities in order to get better prices.

Likewise, they should not forget the principles on copyright exceptions and limitations for libraries listed in a public document published in May 2009 by eIFL.net, IFLA and the Library Copyright Alliance, which includes the most prominent scenarios, namely:

- *Preservation.* A library should allow both published and unpublished studies to be copied for preservation purposes, including migration into different formats.

- *Legal deposit.* Legal deposit laws must be expanded to include documents in all sorts of formats and allow them to be preserved.

- *Interlibrary loan and document supply.* Libraries may supply documents, regardless of their format, for the direct use of other libraries.

- *Education and classroom teaching.* Studies included in the library's collections may be copied to support lecturers in their classes.

- *Reproduction for research or private purposes.* Copies should be allowed for individual use in research and study.

- *Provision for persons with disabilities.* Libraries are authorised to transform their collections to other formats appropriate for disabled persons.

- *General free use exceptions* applicable to libraries.

- *Orphan works.* These are works whose rights have not been identified or located, rendering them logically exempt from copyright.

- *Technological protection measures* that prevent unlawful uses.

Technological issues

Within this section we shall highlight two main issues: the choice of *software and hardware* and *metadata*. With regard to the former, Zhang and Gourley (2008) suggest a fairly complex process for choosing suitable software and hardware in a digitalisation process. The following points should be borne in mind: analysing original materials and the structure of their contents, the types of texts and images they include, their size and location, as well as the relations among the different digital objects; identifying the different kinds of potential users of the collections to be digitalised and their needs; quantifying a real budget that facilitates library decision-making; considering the technological compatibility with the institution's other existing infrastructures; assigning library and computer staff to the project according to their training and technical skills; and last but not least, defining the strategic goals of digitalisation and drawing up a timeline that facilitates staff efforts.

Once these needs have been defined, the next step is to evaluate the different programmes and computers following the criteria suggested by the technical team. There is no need for these criteria to be common to all digitalisation projects, although they will usually be related to the different characteristics of the programmes and computers used for digitalisation. This assessment will help the project leaders choose the most appropriate software, either open source or commercial,[63] and hardware to use when digitalising the different materials.

The second factor to bear in mind within the technical requirements is the choice of the metadata that define the digital objects. The most generic definition of metadata is 'data about data', meaning that this concept alludes to any element that helps to identify, describe and locate electronic resources on the web. There are different kinds of metadata, but three are regarded as fundamental: descriptive metadata, which define the attributes of the digital object like its name, creator, size, etc.; administrative metadata, which include information on the object's location, the user name, rights management, preservation, etc.; and structural metadata, which include factors like the relations among the digital objects. The process of assigning metadata to digital collections is an extremely important part of a digitalisation project in that it facilitates and maximises the accessibility of the collection. Therefore, the decisions taken on the choice of metadata standards and levels of description of these collections depend on the purposes of the organisation, the availability of human and technological resources and users' expectations. For this reason, the metadata chosen for digital collections must meet the following criteria (NISO Framework Working Group, 2007).

- They must adapt to the existing standards[64] and be the most appropriate for the specific materials being digitalised, the patrons of the collection and its current and future uses. It is wise for the library to draw up an inventory of metadata standards with the descriptions and applications of each one in order to choose the most appropriate model for each digital collection.

- They must be interoperable so that all the contents can be compiled and retrieved by other services. The purpose of interoperability is to help users look for and access information housed on different domains and owned by different institutions. The OAI-PHM protocol and metasearch engines, which we have discussed in the chapter on repositories, enhance the interoperability of systems.

- They must use authorities control and content standards to describe and relate digital objects. Controlled terms are usually used to express the attributes of each one: personal names, corporate names, place names, subject names, etc., and each is expressed according to cataloguing rules, controlled vocabularies or thesauruses and classification systems.

- They must include a clear statement of the conditions and terms of use of each digital object, which usually includes factors related to copyright and any restriction on use. PREMIS[65] is a specific scheme of metadata to describe the copyright status of works, ONIX-PL[66] and PLUS License Data Format[67] are used to cite permits and licences of digital collections within the library and XACML[68] is a standard for representing rights languages for workflow.

- They must support the long-term management and preservation of digital objects and describe digital files, including capture information, format, file, size, checksum, etc.

- They must include qualities of good objects and include authority, authenticity, archivability, persistence and unique identification.

Digital preservation policies

As mentioned above, the digital environment has contributed to improving processes and services at libraries, but it has also turned into a breeding ground for certain problems. Even though electronic documents offer easier access to information than traditional ones, their permanence and survival over the years is not yet guaranteed.[69] Today, the preservation of digital materials is an issue yet to be resolved that is of great concern to academia.

Keefer and Gallart (2007) point to three preservation strategies for digital collections which we shall outline below. They stress that libraries tend to use a combination of these methods according to the formats of the resources, their planned uses and the organisation's technical capacity:

- *Refreshing*, or transferring data from one support to another. More than a preservation strategy, this is considered a necessary step as it lowers the risk of data loss due to the deterioration that all physical supports undergo. It offers no solution for protecting information from the risk of technological obsolescence, but it is a necessary step in the preservation process. Furthermore, it requires neither a major investment in equipment nor a high degree of technical knowledge on the part of the staff, so it is easy to implement in all libraries.

- *Migration* is another digital preservation strategy whose purpose is to convert a document created in a given environment and codified in a given format into another format so that it works on a new, more up-to-date or standardised IT platform. This preservation method has several advantages: as it is a proven operation, it requires no specialised technical knowledge, part of the process can be automated, and the trends towards standardisation of software and formats make the job easier and convert the document into a format that is compatible with today's systems. Its disadvantages include the difficulties in programming complex digital objects; with the alteration of the document, you run the risk of losing important features, and the operation needs to be repeated periodically over the resource's lifetime.

- Environment *emulation* is the only strategy that ensures recovery of the original document with no alterations. Its purpose is for computer systems of the future to have the capacity to recover the original data, as if they were the original software. In this way, the emulator programme will allow future users to see the resource just as it was when it was created. This process requires no constant tracking of the resource's format and offers a solution for complex digital objects, as there is no need to control each kind of format and functionality they contain. On the down side, there are still few real experiences, and programming emulators are complex and require expert knowledge, meaning that the cost is high and their usefulness will depend on the predisposition of future professionals.

As mentioned above, digital preservation is a priority issue that has been a concern to the research community for years; as a result, there has been a constant stream of reports, programmes and projects related to this subject. The European initiatives include the DELOS[70] (Digital Preservation Cluster) programme, which began in 2004; the creation of the DCC[71] (Digital Curation Centre) in 2004, which is the leading organisation on conservation and preservation issues; the CASPAR[72] (Cultural, Artistic and Scientific Knowledge for Preservation, Access and Retrieval), DPE[73] (Digital Preservation Europe) and PLANETS[74] (Permanent Long-term Access through Networked Services) programmes, which got underway in 2006 and are still operating today; and finally PARSE.insight[75] (Permanent Access to the Records of Science in Europe), which was launched in 2008.

American experiences include the Library of Congress's NDIIPP[76] (National Digital Information Infrastructure & Preservation Program) and the different avenues of action within RLG/OCLC[77] on preservation activities.

Within the context of university libraries, worth noting are the collection preservation and maintenance department at the Cornell University Library,[78] along with the LOCKSS[79] (Lots of Copies Keep Stuff Safe) programmes developed by Stanford University Libraries and CLOCKSS[80] (*Controlled LOCKSS*), in which libraries from all over the world participate.

Digitisation projects: examples and models

Even though throughout this entire chapter we have re-iterated that one of the most important services offered by university libraries today is access to their own digital collections, it is impossible to survey all the initiatives and experiences to date.[81] Nevertheless, because of their importance, we would like to close this section on user-centred services by talking about three recent massive digitalisation projects which provide open access to hundreds of different kinds of materials and documents:

Google Books[82]: This is the most famous and controversial massive book digitalisation project today. Its purpose, in the words of the company itself, is to 'facilitate the search for relevant books, especially those that cannot be found any other way, such as out-of-print books, without violating authors' and publishers' rights'. It has two main avenues of action. The first is a Library Project, as Google has signed agreements with numerous libraries all over the world[83] to digitalise part of their book collections. The basic information on the digitalised book, and often excerpts from it, can be viewed on Google's search engine. If the book is out of print and exempt from copyright, it can be seen in its entirety. In all cases, links are provided to the online booksellers where the book is sold. Likewise, Google Books also has a Partner Program, which the company extends to publishers and authors to allow them to include their books in the project in order to enhance their visibility. Despite the fact that at first Google Books seemed like the perfect solution for open access to information, the company has suffered from an onslaught of criticisms and sanctions since the project was launched. To cite a recent one, in December 2009 the French court system sentenced Google to a 300,000 euro fine payable to the La Martinière publishing group for having reproduced excerpts of works without its permission.[84]

Europeana[85] was launched in late 2008 as a vast European digital library. It includes six million works of different kinds, including literary texts, reproductions of art works, audiovisual materials and television archives, in 21 languages. The project is financed by the European Commission, and it enjoys heavy backing from the member states, which have earmarked high budgets for it. The affiliated institutions include members that are libraries, museums, archives and other entities that have helped to create Europeana, along with its partners, organisations worldwide that supply the portal with content. The project has already won an Erasmus Award for Networking Europe in 2009 (see Figure 5.7).

The World Digital Library[86] was created in April 2009 by a team of professionals from the United States Library of Congress with the support of UNESCO and the help and financial support of private institutions, companies and foundations from different countries. The project includes digitalised collections of manuscripts, maps, rare books, music scores, recordings, films, engravings, photographs and blueprints. The World Digital Library interface has a unique, highly original design for accessing the information, as the constituent documents are grouped by countries, as well as by period, subject, kind of document and partner institution. All of this is supplemented with personalised descriptions of each document and interviews with the conservators on important materials. The browsing tools and content descriptions are

Figure 5.7 Europeana

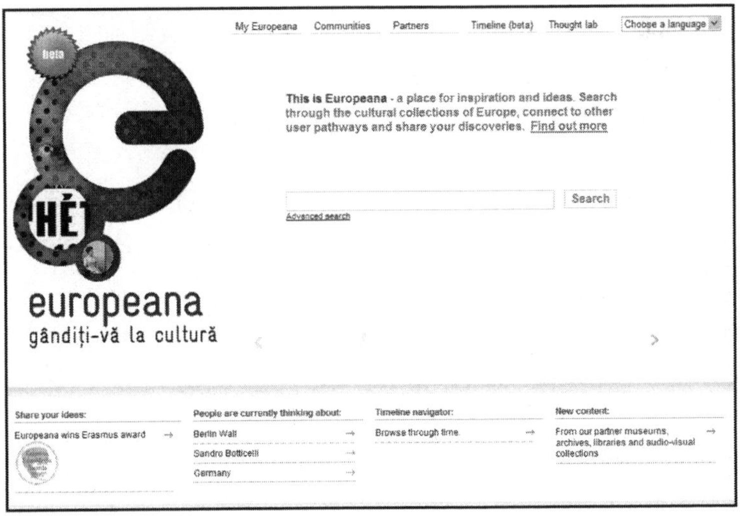

available in Arabic, Chinese, English, French, Portuguese, Russian and Spanish.

2.0 tools

Web 2.0, Library 2.0

In 2005, Tim O'Reilly defined Web 2.0, also called the social web, as the 'business revolution in the computer industry caused by the move to the Internet as a platform and an attempt to understand the rules for success on that new platform'. There are many other definitions of Web 2.0 that describe it as follows (O'Reilly, 2005; Anderson, 2007; Kelly et al., 2009):

- It developed based on the advent of a new generation of web-related technologies and standards such as Ajax (Asynchronous JavaScript and XML), used to create interactive applications; SOAP (Simple Object Access Protocol), devoted to integrating information services; REST (Representational State Transfer), which is used to develop web services, microformats that enable semantic meaning to be aggregated onto different types of content; and open APIs (Application Programming Interfaces), which makes it possible for websites to interact with each other.

- Simplicity for users to create contents and develop their own services without the need for specific programming knowledge.

- Transparency, participation, cooperation and reuse of all the information generated by users: the overarching principle of Web 2.0.

- Interoperability between systems and the capacity to integrate and share services and resources.

- As the web is regarded as a platform, all the services generated on it are externally hosted so users can access them from any computer with an Internet hook-up without the need to belong to a given organisation or entity.

The upshot of the first meetings where the Web 2.0 concept was discussed was the comparison between Web 1.0 and Web 2.0 seen in Figure 5.8. It is an indisputable fact that the services and products generated in both systems are distinct and that their evolution in 2.0 reveals a change in the web paradigm.

In addition to promoting the growth and progress of services, the development of the web has entailed a change in attitude and thinking not just in technology but in many sectors. Thus, we now talk here about Science 2.0,[87] Education 2.0, University 2.0, Enterprise 2.0 and Library 2.0.[88] One of the most widely accepted definitions of the concept of Library 2.0 was contributed by Casey and Savastinuk (2006): 'The heart of

Figure 5.8 Web 1.0 and Web 2.0 compared

Web 1.0		Web 2.0
DoubleClick	-->	Google AdSense
Ofoto	-->	Flickr
Akamai	-->	BitTorrent
mp3.com	-->	Napster
Britannica Online	-->	Wikipedia
personal Websites	-->	blogging
evite	-->	upcoming.org and EVDB
domain name speculation	-->	search engine optimisation
page views	-->	cost per click
screen scraping	-->	Web services
publishing	-->	participation
content management systems	-->	wikis
directories (taxonomy)	-->	tagging ("folksonomy")
stickiness	-->	syndication

Library 2.0 is user-centered change. It is a model for library service that encourages constant and purposeful change, inviting user participation in the creation of both the physical and the virtual services they want, supported by consistently evaluating services. It also attempts to reach new users and better serve current ones through improved customer-driven offerings'. Along the same lines, Blyberg (2006) justifies the existence and importance of Library 2.0 (L2) through eleven principles:

- L2 is partially a response to a post-Google world.

- L2 requires internal reorganisation.

- L2 requires a fundamental change in a library's mission.

- L2 requires a fundamental change in how we handle 'authority'.

- L2 requires technological agility.

- L2 challenges library orthodoxy on almost every level.

- L2 requires a radical change in the way ILSs and vendors work.

- L2 both enables and requires libraries to work together.

- L2 is actually happening.

- L2 is revolutionary.

- L2 is essential for survival/belonging.

This list reveals the deep-seated change brought about by the onset of the 2.0 revolution in library services. Patrons are no longer satisfied with the traditional services that libraries have offered until now, the methods and working tools are no longer the same, and information professionals have to experiment with the new emerging technologies. These changes are not always welcomed by professionals, so the arrival of Library 2.0 has been received unevenly in different organisations. To help all the less experienced professionals who see technology as a handicap for their growth and development, we would like to cite two initiatives being spearheaded by librarians: *A Guide to Using Web 2.0 in Libraries*[89] published by the Scottish Library and Information Council (SLIC) in December 2009, and *A Librarian's 2.0 Manifesto*[90] written by Laura B. Cohen and published on her blog in 2006. The guide aims to highlight the benefits of Web 2.0 for library services; these benefits include reaching a wider audience, serving a larger number and wider variety of patrons, enabling services with added value to be developed, making professional development possible and enhancing the library's promotion and marketing. The guide also includes testimonials from professionals singing the praises of Library 2.0, case studies, documents to help readers use 2.0 tools, recommendations to bear in mind when deciding to implement it and forms where libraries can send in examples of practical uses.

The manifesto, in turn, discusses some of the principles that should guide the actions of a 2.0 librarian:

- To recognise that the universe of information culture is changing fast and that libraries need to respond positively to these changes to provide resources and services that users need and want.
- To educate about the information culture of the users.
- Not to be defensive about the library, but to look clearly at its situation and make an honest assessment about what can be accomplished.
- To become an active participant in moving the library forward.
- To recognise that libraries change slowly, and work with colleagues to expedite the responsiveness to change.

- To be courageous about proposing new services and new ways of providing services, even though some colleagues will be resistant.

- To enjoy the excitement and fun of positive change and convey this to colleagues and users.

- To take an experimental approach to change and be willing to make mistakes.

- Not to wait until something is perfect before releasing it.

- Not to fear Google or related services, but rather to take advantage of these services to benefit users while also providing excellent library services that users need.

- To be willing to go where users are, both online and in physical spaces, to practise the profession.

- To create open websites that allows users to join with librarians to contribute content in order to enhance their learning experience and provide assistance to their peers.

- To lobby for an open catalogue that provides personalised, interactive features that users expect in online information environments.

- To encourage the library's administration to blog.

2.0 tools and their application in university libraries

Perhaps because of their degree of specialisation, university libraries were the first to begin developing 2.0 services for their patrons. Internal library tasks have also been affected by the new technologies introduced by the new web, justifying the idea that 2.0 applications know no bounds. Figure 5.9 shows several examples of the vast number of tools and resources that the social web has devised for its users: blogs, wikis, RSS feeds, social networks and many others. Below

Figure 5.9 2.0 tools

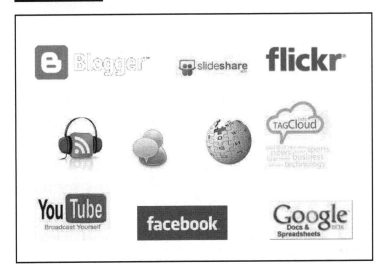

we shall discuss these tools and analyse their application in the different processes and services offered by university libraries.

Blogs

Blogs are theme-based websites that are extremely easy to make. They enable users to interact with each other constantly through the comments and opinions that they post. All blogs must be constantly updated as that determines how topical and timely this tool can be. There are more than 55,000 blogs on the web[91] on all imaginable topics, and they are one of the most widely used 2.0 resources in university libraries all over the world. The widespread use of blogs in library services is largely due to the existence of free programmes that make it easy to create them, coupled with the low level of technological knowledge needed to develop a blog. Wordpress,[92] Blogger[93] and Live Journal[94] are free, external applications that require no previous installation, just registration in a system through which each user gets a username and password that let them manage the blog from any computer with an Internet hook-up.

Within a university library, blogs can be used for many different purposes:

- As a specific website for each thematic library or faculty, should the library service be decentralised; blogs are usually designed as complementary to the library service's main website.

- As a channel of communication between users and professionals or among librarians working in different departments.

- As an electronic platform for each event (workshops, conventions and assemblies) held at the library. A blog can serve as a log posting reports on the daily proceedings of the event.

- As a visual bulletin board and newsletter of the library managed and updated by the librarians with the motto 'at least one news item every day'. This initiative facilitates visibility, promotes the service and keeps the entire university community apprised of the latest developments at the library.

Just to cite one of the many examples of blogs at university libraries today, the librarians at the North Carolina State University Library[95] have a blog that falls within the last category listed above. The news items posted on this blog are extremely varied and range from new product displays to profiles of the staff working at the library.

Wikis

'They are *Websites* that allow the easy creation and editing of any number of *interlinked Web pages* via *Web browser*'.[96]

Wikipedia is the most popular and well-known application of this tool, a web project whose goal is to develop a free encyclopaedia through user participation and contributions. Wikipedia has become an extremely important source of information that is consulted quite frequently, and its growth is unstoppable despite the fact that some unfavourable criticism has been levelled at it.[97] For example, the results of a survey administered to 68 high-tech professionals about how they use and share information from Wikipedia for work purposes revealed that these experts view it as a general source of reference information, but one that is not very rigorous, that is still under development and whose editorial process needs improvement. As a result, these professionals expressed little interest in contributing information to it (Chen, 2009).

Wikis are not one of the 2.0 resources most frequently used in university libraries, despite the fact that just like with blogs, free services like Wikispaces[98] and Wikia[99] are used to create and host them. A study conducted in 2009 on the use of wikis in this kind of library reveals that of the 48 respondents,[100] only 16 use this tool for their work, four have tried it, 13 are planning to use it and 15 have no intention of using it. According to this analysis (Chu, 2009), the main reasons why these libraries use wikis are the following:

- to facilitate the co-construction of web pages;
- to enhance information sharing among librarians;
- to archive different versions of work online;
- to speed up the updating of web pages.

In addition to these practical applications, wikis are taking shape as the ideal 2.0 tool for teamwork. They enable librarians to share their work, facilitating jobs like editing, creating and eliminating contents. If a university uses a decentralised model in which each faculty or school has its own library, wikis can be extremely helpful in technical jobs, cataloguing, subject standardisation and classification, or in drawing up thematic guides, as some of the faculties at the University of Seville, Spain,[101] have done. There, they use wikis to keep compilations of electronic or printed information resources related to the courses taught at the university. They are constantly growing, being revised and updated, they support the courses and their goal is to gather opinions and suggestions from members of the university community in order to further enrich the contents.

Social networks

These are shared websites whose main goal is for registered users to share information. Generally speaking, the most famous networks are Facebook[102] and Myspace,[103] but there are also others used in more restricted or professional spheres, like Linkedin,[104] Xing[105] and Viadeo.[106] These tools are very popular and heavily used, but they have also been the subject of criticism about the lack of privacy in certain cases. For this reason, all users of social networks must be aware of the dangers and risks involved and must be trained in how to use them correctly.

The main uses of social networks in university libraries are to serve first as a channel of dissemination and marketing of the libraries' products and services, and secondly as a means of communication among professionals from different regions and countries. There is no doubt that Facebook is the network that the majority of libraries choose to promote themselves.[107] Most of them create a profile containing their basic information and photographs, and then they use the profile to announce events, special hours, news, job offers, interruptions in any service, statistics, catalogue searches, article database searches, metasearches and any other new development in the library setting. The most original Facebook applications are the ones spotlighted by Boyer and Ryan in the 2009 DLF Spring Forum:[108] a clickable map to notify friends of the physical location of Swem Library at the College of William and Mary (Williamsburg, Virginia), Eastern Illinois University's Live Reference Chat and an application designed by North Carolina State University Libraries to help students meet up in physical library space for planned or ad hoc activities, such as group study sessions. The application provides an 'at a glance' view of all activities in the library, activities by the users' friends and useful library information, such as hours and study room availability. Users can join activities created by others, or can simply broadcast their own activity to the community.

Content syndication

According to the definition by Rodríguez Gairín et al. (2006: 214), 'Syndication is the process whereby a producer or distributor of contents on Internet provides these contents to a subscriber or to a network of subscribers'. This is a way of distributing information, making it more accessible and also allowing for alerts and updates without the need to constantly browse the Internet. This redistribution mainly takes place in two formats: *RSS* (Really Simple Syndication) feeds and *Atom*. In order for content syndication to be possible, a compatible reader and web browser are needed. There is a wide range of RSS readers, but they can all be classified into three categories:

- Desktop aggregators or readers like FeedReader,[109] RSSReader[110] and RSSOwl[111] which are installed on the users' computer.

- Online aggregators or readers like Bloglines[112] and Google Reader,[113] which do not need a local installation; all you have to do to use them is register on their website.

- Aggregators or readers included as plug-ins on browsers like Firefox, Nestcape and Opera.

Content syndication has been widely accepted in university libraries[114] and serves a variety of functions, including:

- Alerts on new additions to the library catalogue. For years the channel of communication that libraries used to announce their new acquisitions was e-mail; at the beginning of every week or month, the library professional had to remember to send an updated file containing the new catalogue items. With content syndication, each library user can receive this information automatically without the librarian having to do anything.

- Alerts on all the new developments at the library: new product acquisitions, special hours, launches of new services, etc.

- Alerts on documents published in e-journals and databases to which the library has subscribed, so that users can receive all the relevant updates without the need for them to visit the journal websites every time a new issue is published.

Many university libraries have implemented services of this kind on their web portals or blogs. Just to cite a few examples, the University of Oklahoma Libraries offers its users the option of subscribing to library news via RSS. This news is categorised in three ways: by collection, subject or title.[115] Likewise, the University of Saskatchewan Library in Canada proposes content syndication for the e-journals to which it subscribes.[116]

Social bookmarking

Social bookmarking, also called tagging, is another Web 2.0 tool used to store links on the Internet with the goal of sharing them. In this way, each user can share their own resources and benefit from those compiled by others. The advantages that Grey (2005) attributes to this social tool are listed below:

- Storing key links on the net vs. on a local computer – allows access from any machine at any time.

- A fast and very effective way to keep track of stuff – this means you are not waiting for the Google spider to visit any longer. You can get a RSS ping as soon as a link is added.

- Examining tags per link gives you a feel for how the rest of the world sees things vs. your private ontology.

- Using a 'secret' group tag allows group members to alert each other of key links.

- Applying 'flat' tags (single words) is far more flexible than operating within a hierarchy of folders (facetted classification).

Del.icio.us[117] is perhaps the most widely used service to collectively manage social bookmarks at university libraries.[118] It has been up and running since 2003 and has a user-friendly interface, as it enables bookmarks originally stored on browsers to be added and organised through a system of tags. Gallart (2009) claims that social bookmarks are used in libraries to achieve the following goals:

- to retrieve and save valuable information that unexpectedly emerges;

- to access the links chosen from any computer with an Internet hook-up and share them with colleagues and users;

- to gather thematic resources of interest;
- to develop compilations of links quickly and effectively;
- to expand information of interest by browsing through other tags.

The same author also points to several stumbling blocks:

- excess information;
- most followers are strangers;
- no statistics on use.

File-sharing

This includes a group of tools aimed at hosting and sharing different kinds of digital artefacts such as documents, photographs, videos, presentations and recordings. They are free social services as they allow users to send comments, opinions and ratings. Just like the tools discussed above, there is a variety of solutions that make this shared information management possible, but the most successful ones are GoogleDocs[119] for documents, which enables users to create, edit, publish and share different contents in different kinds of office documents; YouTube,[120] a highly popular service where you can upload and share videos; SlideShare[121] for presentations; and Flickr[122] for photographs.

Some libraries, especially in the United States, are beginning to use these websites to complement their face-to-face services, to offer new services or simply to seek new avenues of communication with their patrons. The majority of the experiences are virtual tours of the library, such as the videos posted on YouTube from the University Library at Wisconsin-Stout[123] and the Tour of Library West at the University of Florida,[124] where all the library services are shown along with an explanation of each service by the person in charge. However, delving a bit further, these tools are also perfect for sharing virtual exhibitions and for providing user training and library orientation every academic year.

Open-source/social software

These are computer applications which can be freely used, copied, studied, changed and redistributed, plus they are also classified as social, similar to the ones described above, as they include a variety of options of sharing and collaborating with other users. With the advent of Web 2.0, many library jobs and tools have been improved with new solutions that facilitate the job of professionals. This is the case of integrated library management systems (ILS),[125] more specifically the OPAC module,[126] reference managers, content management systems and e-learning platforms.

Bibliographic reference managers are extremely useful tools for university libraries that enormously facilitate the work of researchers. They enable users to create their own bibliographic databases by adding items or by importing the references found after checking databases. They also allow users to organise their own personal bibliography, draw up bibliographic lists which are automatically formatted correctly for inclusion in any study, insert citations into a document being written and share bibliographic reference files with other colleagues and publish them on the web. Zotero[127] and Mendeley[128] are open-source reference management applications that use 2.0 features and utilities such as social networks to share files with other researchers working on similar subjects, plus they are compatible with products and services from the social web like YouTube and Flickr. Likewise, CiteULike[129] and Connotea[130] are social reference managers that pursue the same goal as the aforementioned ones, storing millions of citations from research documents for each user that are visible to all users. CiteULike includes services like CiteGeist, which shows the most popular references in recent days, and Watchlist, which offers users tracking lists to show shared interests and to stay abreast of the new documents that each user is reading.

Content management systems (CMS) are applications that help users edit and manage information through a web browser. In addition to offering a clear, simple administrative system through which all the web contents are managed, they also include a variety of 2.0 utilities: blogs, surveys, news channels, ratings and comments through tags, etc., which make them a social tool in which users shift from being mere spectators to actively providing content. Joomla[131] and Drupal[132] are two solutions used in university libraries to implement the institutional website or intranet. The University of León (Spain) has implemented its corporate website with Joomla, while the University of Minnesota Libraries has designed the website of its Biomedical Library using Drupal.[133]

E-learning platforms are used at university libraries for virtual user training to complement face-to-face training. They are dynamic learning environments aimed at facilitating the teaching/learning process. Prominent examples of e-learning platforms include Moodle (Modular Object Oriented Dynamic Learning Environment),[134] which has been implemented at many universities all over the world, and Sakai,[135] which began to be used in the United States but has quickly expanded to other parts of the world. Both solutions allow 2.0 tools to be included like blogs, wikis, discussion forums and RSS channels, which make them more open and interactive. Just to cite several examples of university libraries that use Moodle, the Carleton College Library offers library resources that can be included in the courses in which students are enrolled via Moodle,[136] and The London School of Economics and Political Science of the University of London and the Library User Education Team portal complements face-to-face training.

Technological advances pave the way for the advent of new web-related concepts which are extensions of the web. In this chapter, we have spoken about Web 2.0, which entails user involvement in content creation as opposed to just content consumption. Yet new web developments are also in the works, including Web 3.0, where information is semantic in nature and can be interpreted by both humans and machines, and Web 4.0, in which intelligent personal agents and distributed search will come to the forefront.

Notes

1. *http://portal.unesco.org/ci/en/files/19636/11228863531Prague Declaration.pdf/PragueDeclaration.pdf*
2. *http://archive.ifla.org/III/wsis/BeaconInfSoc.html*
3. *http://archive.ifla.org/VII/s42/pub/IL-guidelines2004-e.pdf*
4. *http://archive.ifla.org/VII/s42/pub/IL-Guidelines2006.pdf*
5. *http://www.acrl.org/ala/mgrps/divs/acrl/issues/infolit/ index.cfm*
6. *http://www.sconul.ac.uk/groups/information_literacy/papers/ Seven_pillars2.pdf*
7. *http://www.mariapinto.es/alfineees/AlfinEEES.htm*
8. *http://www.alfared.org*
9. At many universities, students attending these specialised courses can earn academic credit for them, leading them to gain interest within the student community.
10. A service offered by the Malmö University Library (Sweden). People can book a librarian for a free individual 60 minute session of guided information searching *http://www.mah.se/ english/Library/Services/Book-a-Librarian*
11. *http://arxiv.org*
12. The e-prints are preliminary digital versions of a work that the author intends to send to a formal journal, but that are previously distributed among a group of departments or

colleagues who are working in the same area of interest, firstly with the aim of receiving reviews, comments and suggestions, and secondly, of announcing the trends and results of the research that he/she is developing.

13. *http://repec.org*

14. *http://cogprints.org*

15. *http://repositories.webometrics.info/top400_rep_es.asp*

16. Software developed essentially for the implementation of digital repositories *http://www.eprints.org/software/*

17. They are Harnad and Suber's answers about a question asked by Remedios Melero. She disseminates them in 1st Conference of Os-repositories (Zaragoza, Spain, 2006).

18. *http://www.eprints.org/openaccess/policysignup*

19. October 2009.

20. *http://www.nih.gov/*

21. *http://www.pubmedcentral.nih.gov/*

22. *http://www.harvard.edu/*

23. *http://web.mit.edu/*

24. *http://oa.mpg.de/openaccess-berlin/berlindeclaration.html*

25. October 2009.

26. *http://www.oacompact.org/*

27. Repository directories on a worldwide scale. *http://roar. eprints.org/;http://www.opendoar.org/*

28. *http://eprints.nottingham.ac.uk/policies.html*

29. *http://www.lib.berkeley.edu/brii/*

30. *http://www.hsl.unc.edu/scholcom/OAFundAnnounce.cfm; http://www.library.wisc.edu/scp/openaccess/oafund.html*

31. *http://www.sherpa.ac.uk/*

32. It is what authors call 'interoperability'.

33. OAIster *http://www.oaister.org* and Scientific Commons *http://www.scientificcommons.org* are repository content aggregators or collectors.

34. *http://www.openarchives.org/*

35. *http://www.openarchives.org/*

36. *http://etd.tamu.edu/*

37. Google Scholar *http://scholar.google.com* and Scirus *http://www.scirus.com* are academic search engines. In 2006 Microsoft released its Live Search Academic, which was withdrawn in 2008. This multinational launched in 2009 another scholar

search engine very similar to the previous one *http://academic. research.microsoft.com/*

38. *http://www.jisc.ac.uk/*

39. *http://www.sherpa.ac.uk/*

40. Digital Repositories Programme, which remained until 2008, and Repositories and Preservation Programme, which is still operative, are two of the programmes released by JISC about digital repositories. SHERPA displays its services, resources and projects on the home page of its web.

41. JISC was one of the organisers of the International Repositories Workshop, held in the Netherlands in March 2009.

42. *http://www.surf.nl/en/Pages/home.aspx*

43. To cite only a few projects: LOREnet *http://www.lorenet.nl/ nl/page/luzi/show?showcase=1* is a repository network of teaching materials, and DAREnet, a repository network created in 2004, but that from 2008 became part of NARCIS *http://www.narcis.info/index* a Dutch scientific and academic portal.

44. It is worth mentioning the census of institutional repositories in the United States, under the umbrella of the MIRACLE project (Markey et al., 2007), the report on Open Access in the Nordic countries (Hedlund and Rabow, 2007), the study on the European situation of the institutional repositories (van Eijndhoven and van der Graaf, 2007), the analysis of the repositories in Australia (Kennan and Kingsley, 2009) and in Spain, the report made by Melero et al. in 2009.

45. The Dublin Core began in a meeting held in Dublin (Ohio) in 1995, and was conceived with a view to describe Internet resources and as a response to the need of creating a common standard of metadata. It consists of fifteen description elements of electronic documents (title, creator, subject, description, publisher, contributor, date, type, format, identifier, language, source, relation, coverage, rights), which provide the basic information about them. http://dublincore.org/ The Qualified Dublin Core is an extension of the Dublin Core, where some of its elements are accompanied by a qualifier, which makes them more restrictive (e.g. Date.Created, Date.Available, Date.Modified) *http://dublincore.org/documents/2000/07/11/ dcmes-qualifiers/*

46. *http://www.idealliance.org/industry_resources/intelligent_
content_informed_workflow/prism*
47. *http://www.loc.gov/standards/mods/*
48. *http://www.loc.gov/standards/mets/*
49. This method is proposed in order to minimise efforts on the part of the author when placing contents in a repository. If the information relative to the researchers of their curricula, lists of publications and other services is collected, then the librarian will take part in the self-archive and the author will have to work less.
50. A process through which analogical contents are turned into a sequence of ones and zeros, known as binary code, so that a computer can read them (Hughes, 2004).
51. These are reduced reproductions of documents that require a reader or projector to be viewed.
52. *http://prestospace.org/*
53. *http://europa.eu/legislation_summaries/information_society/
l24226g_es.htm*
54. *http://cordis.europa.eu/fp7/home_es.html*
55. *http://www.dlorg.eu/*
56. *http://www.prestoprime.eu/*
57. *http://dltj.org/article/ala-oitp-digital-proposal/*
58. To cite just a few examples: Good Practice Guide for Developers of Cultural Heritage, a website made in 2004 by UKOLN and Arts and Humanities Data Service and the University of Bath and updated in 2008. Also: Framework of Guidance for Building Good Digital Collections, prepared by the NISO Framework Working Group with support from the Institute of Museum and Library Services, the third edition of which dates from December 2007.
59. 163 countries have signed the convention *http://www.
worldcopyrightcenter.com/signatories-berne-convention.html*
60. *http://www.wipo.int/treaties/es/ip/berne/trtdocs_wo001.html*
61. According to the Berne Convention, the minimum is the author's lifetime plus another 50 years.
62. Creative Commons licences are one of the best-known examples: *http://creativecommons.org*
63. To cite just one example, OCLC's CONTENTdm (*http://www.
contentdm.org/*) and Greenstone, the latter developed for the New Zealand Digital Library Project at the University of

Waikato (*http://www.greenstone.org/*), are two programmes often used to create digital collections.

64. Dublin Core, RDF, EAD, TEI and MODS are just some of the models used to describe digital collections.

65. *http://www.loc.gov/standards/premis/*

66. *http://www.editeur.org/21/ONIX-PL/*

67. *http://www.useplus.com/useplus/license.asp*

68. *http://www.oasis-open.org/committees/tc_home.php?wg_abbrev=xacml*

69. The flimsiness of physical supports and technological obsolescence are the main threats to digital collections, so digital preservation aims to conserve both facets of the document: the physical part and its contents.

70. *http://www.dpc.delos.info/*

71. *http://www.dcc.ac.uk/*

72. *http://www.casparpreserves.eu/*

73. *http://www.digitalpreservationeurope.eu/*

74. *http://www.planets-project.eu/*

75. *http://www.parse-insight.eu/project.php*

76. *http://www.digitalpreservation.gov/*

77. *http://www.oclc.org/digitalpreservation/resources/default.htm*

78. *http://www.library.cornell.edu/preservation/index.html*

79. *http://www.lockss.org/lockss/Home*

80. *http://www.clockss.org/clockss/Home*

81. Dmoz is a fairly up-to-date directory of digital collections *http://www.dmoz.org/Reference/Libraries/Digital/*

82. *http://books.google.com/*

83. All the libraries associated with the project appear on its website, including several university libraries: *http://books.google.com/googlebooks/partners.html*

84. This news item appeared in the online newspaper Elmundo.es on Friday 18 December 2009 *http://www.elmundo.es/elmundo/2009/12/18/navegante/1261141624.html*

85. *http://www.europeana.eu*

86. *http://www.wdl.org/en/*

87. With Science 2.0 there is a change in both researchers' aptitudes and the way information is written and disseminated. Scientific communication is enriched by the appearance of new methods of storage and publication.

88. All the 2.0 concepts share the same characteristics as those listed for Web 2.0 at the beginning of this chapter.

89. *http://www.slainte.org.uk/files/pdf/Web2/Web2GuidelinesFinal.pdf*

90. *http://liblogs.albany.edu/library20/2006/11/a_librarians_20_manifesto.html*

91. Blog directory of Technorati: *http://technorati.com/blogs/directory.*

92. *http://wordpress.com/*

93. *https://www.blogger.com/start?hl=es*

94. *http://www.livejournal.com/*

95. *http://news.lib.ncsu.edu/*

96. Definition extracted from Wikipedia *http://es.wikipedia.org/wiki/Wiki*

97. Among academic researchers, Wikipedia is not regarded as a highly reliable source.

98. *http://www.wikispaces.com/*

99. *http://www.wikia.com/wiki/Wikia*

100. The respondents are academic libraries in several regions around the world: Australia, China, Hong Kong, Singapore, New Zealand and the United States.

101. *http://bib.us.es/aprendizaje_investigacion/guias_tutoriales/*

102. *http://www.facebook.com*

103. *http://www.myspace.com*

104. *http://www.linkedin.com/*

105. *http://www.xing.com*

106. *http://www.viadeo.com*

107. One example of this is the 1,234 members belonging to the group 'Libraries using Facebook pages'. Figure retrieved on 16 January 2010.

108. *http://www.diglib.org/forums/spring2009/*

109. *http://www.feedreader.com*

110. *http://www.rssreader.com*

111. *http://www.rssowl.org*

112. *http://www.bloglines.com*

113. *http://www.google.com/reader*

114. There is a search engine for blogs and RSS channels specialising in libraries called Libworm, *http://www.libworm.com*; it is classified by subject and category.

115. *http://libraries.ou.edu/rss*

116. *http://library.usask.ca/ejournals/rss_title/A*
117. *http://delicious.com*
118. List of libraries that use Del.icio.us to share bookmarks. Most of them classify the links by library subjects or jobs, depending on whether the service is used internally or is for users.
119. *http://docs.google.com*
120. *http://www.youtube.com*
121. *http://www.slideshare.net*
122. *http://www.flickr.com*
123. *http://www.youtube.com/watch?v=S6SSJsQloGg*
124. *http://www.youtube.com/watch?v=i4n2qauQUtM&feature= related*
125. Koha *http://koha.org/* is an example of an open-source, social ILS as it includes tools in some of its modules.
126. We have addressed this point in the chapter on catalogues.
127. *http://www.zotero.org*
128. *http://www.mendeley.com*
129. *http://www.citeulike.org*
130. *http://www.connotea.org*
131. *http://www.joomlaspanish.org*
132. *http://drupal.org*
133. *http://www.biomed.lib.umn.edu*
134. *http://moodle.org*
135. *http://sakaiproject.org*
136. *http://apps.carleton.edu/campus/library/for_faculty/faculty_ working/libe_moodle*

References

ACRL/ALA (2000) *Information Literacy Competency Standards for Higher Education.* Available from: *http://www.ala.org/ala/mgrps/divs/acrl/standards/ informationliteracycompetency.cfm.*

ACRL (2003) *Characteristics of Programs of Information Literacy that Illustrate Best Practices: A Guideline.* Available from: *http://www.ala.org/ala/mgrps/divs/acrl/ standards/characteristics.cfm.*

ALA's Office for Information Technology Policy (2007) *Draft Principles for Digitized Content*. Available from: *http://dltj.org/article/ala-oitp-digital-proposal*.

Anderson, P. (2007) 'What is Web 2.0? Ideas, technologies and implications for education', *JISC Technology & Standards Watch*. Available from: *http://www.jisc.ac.uk/media/documents/techwatch/tsw0701b.pdf*.

Bainton, T. (2001) 'Information literacy and academic libraries: The SCONUL approach (UK/Ireland)', *Proceedings of the 67th IFLA Council and General Conference*. Available from: *http://archive.ifla.org/IV/ifla67/papers/016-126e.pdf*.

Blyberg, J. (2006) *11 reason why Library 2.0 exists and matters*. Available from: *http://www.blyberg.net/2006/01/09/11-reasons-why-library-20-exists-and-matters*.

Boyer, J. and Ryan, J. (2009) 'Considering Facebook in the library', *Proceedings of the Digital Library Federation, Spring Forum*. Available from: *http://www.diglib.org/forums/spring2009/presentations/Boyer.pdf*.

Brown, S. and Swan, A. (2007) *Researchers' use of academic libraries and their services, a report by the Research Information Network and the Consortium of Research Libraries*. Available from: *http://eprints.ecs.soton.ac.uk/13868/1/libraries-report-2007.pdf*.

Casey, M. and Savastinuk, L.C. (2006) 'Library 2.0: Service for the next-generation library'. *Library Journal*. Available from: *http://www.libraryjournal.com/article/CA6365200.html*.

Catts, R. and Lau, J. (2008) *Towards Information Literacy Indicators*. Paris: UNESCO. Available from: *http://www.uis.unesco.org/template/pdf/cscl/InfoLit.pdf*.

Chen, H.L. (2009) 'The use and sharing of information from Wikipedia by high-tech professionals for work purposes', *The Electronic Library*, 27(6): 893–905.

Chu, S.K.-W. (2009) 'Using wikis in academic libraries', *Journal of Academic Librarianship*, 35(2): 170–6.

Cohen, L. (2006) *A Librarian's 2.0 Manifesto*. Available from: *http://liblogs.albany.edu/library20/2006/11/a_librarians_20_manifesto.html*.

Crow, R. (2002) *The Case for Institutional Repositories: A SPARC Position Paper*. Available from: *http://www.arl.org/sparc/bm~doc/ir_final_release_102.pdf*.

Cuevas Cerveró, A. (2007) *Lectura, alfabetización en información y biblioteca escolar*. Gijón: Trea.

Echeverria, M. and Barredo, P. (2005) 'Online journals: Their impact on document delivery', *Interlending & Document Supply*, 33(3): 145–9.

Egan, N. (2005) 'The impact of electronic full-text resources on inter-library loan: A ten year study at John Jay College of Criminal Justice', *Journal of Interlibrary Loan, Document Delivery and Electronic Reserve*, 15(3): 23–41.

eIFL.net (2009) *Handbook on Copyright and Related Issues for Libraries*. Available from: *http://www.eifl.net/cps/sections/services/eifl-ip/issues/handbook/handbook-complete-text/downloadFile/file/handbook2009_en.pdf?nocache=1256507140.35*.

Gallart, N. (2009) *Delicious en la Biblioteca Universitaria de Sabadell UAB*. Available from: *http://comunidad20.sedic.es/?p=278*.

Goodier, R. and Dean, E. (2004) 'Changing patterns in interlibrary loan and document supply', *Interlending & Document Supply*, 32(4): 206–14.

Grey, D. (2005) *Social Bookmarking – More Than Meets the Eye*. Available from: *http://denham.typepad.com/km/2005/01/social_bookmark.html*.

Hames, I. (2007) *Peer Review and Manuscript Management in Scientific Journals: Guidelines for Good Practice*. Malden: Blackwell.

Harnad, S. and McGovern, N. (2009) 'Institutional repository success is dependent upon mandates', *Bulletin of the American Society for Information Science and Technology*, 35(4). Available from: *http://www.asis.org/Bulletin/Apr-09/AprMay09_Harnad-McGovern.pdf.*

Hazen, D., Horrell J. and Merrill-Oldham, J. (1998) *Selecting Research Collections for Digitization.* Available from: *http://www.clir.org/pubs/reports/hazen/pub74.html.*

Hedlund, T. and Rabow, I. (2007) *Open Access in the Nordic Countries: A State of the Art Report.* Available from: *http://www.nordforsk.org/_img/oa_report_020707.pdf.*

Hernández Pérez, T., Rodríguez Mateos, D. and Bueno de la Fuente, G. (2007) 'Open Access: El papel de las bibliotecas en los repositorios institucionales de acceso abierto', *Anales de Documentación*, 10. Available from: *http://revistas.um.es/analesdoc/article/viewFile/1141/1191.*

Horwood, L. et al. (2004) 'OAI compliant institutional repositories and the role of library staff', *Library Management*, 25(4/5): 170–6.

Hughes, L.M. (2004) *Digitizing Collections: Strategic Issues for the Information Manager.* London: Facet.

Joint, N. (2008) 'Is digitisation the new circulation?: Borrowing trends, digitisation and the nature of reading in US and UK libraries', *Library Review*, 57(2): 86–95.

Joint, N. (2009) 'Choosing between print or digital collection building in times of financial constraint', *Library Review*, 58(4): 264–71.

Jones, C. (2007) *Institutional Repositories: Content and Culture in an Open Access Environment.* Oxford: Chandos, pp. 14–23.

Keefer, A. and Gallart, N. (2007) *La preservación de recursos digitales: El reto para las bibliotecas del siglo XXI.* Barcelona: UOC.

Kelly, B. et al. (2009) 'Library 2.0: Balancing the risks and benefits to maximise the dividends', *Program: Electronic Library and Information Systems*, 43(3): 311–27.

Kennan, M.A. and Kingsley, D. (2009) 'The state of the nation: A snapshot of Australian institutional repositories', *First Monday*, 14(2). Available from: *http://firstmonday.org/htbin/cgiwrap/bin/ojs/index.php/fm/article/viewArticle/2282/2092*.

Labastida Juan, I. and Iglesias Rebollo, C. (2006) *Guía sobre gestión de derechos de autor y acceso abierto en bibliotecas, servicios de documentación y archivos*. Madrid: SEDIC. Available from: *http://www.sedic.es/dchos_autor_normaweb.01.07.pdf*.

Lau, J. (2006) *Guidelines on Information Literacy for Lifelong Learning*. Veracruz, Mexico: IFLA. Available from: *http://archive.ifla.org/VII/s42/pub/IL-Guidelines2006.pdf*.

Lynch, C.A. (2003) 'Institutional repositories: Essential infrastructure for scholarship in the Digital Age', *ARL: Bimonthly report*, No. 226. Available from: *http://www.arl.org/resources/pubs/br/br226/br226ir.shtml*.

Mark, T. and Shearer, K. (2006) 'Institutional repositories: A review of content recruitment strategies', *World Library and Information Congress: 72nd IFLA General Conference and Council*. Available from: *http://archive.ifla.org/IV/ifla72/papers/155-Mark_Shearer-en.pdf*.

Markey, K. et al. (2007) *Census of Institutional Repositories in the United States: MIRACLE Project Research Findings*. Available from: *http://www.clir.org/pubs/reports/pub140/pub140.pdf*.

Marti, M.C. et al. (2008) 'Alfabetización digital: Un peldaño hacia la sociedad de la información', *Medicina y Seguridad del Trabajo*, 54(210). Available from: *http://scielo.isciii.es/pdf/mesetra/v54n210/especial2.pdf*.

Melero, R. et al. (2009) *Situación de los repositorios institucionales en España: Informe 2009*. Available from: *http://digital.csic.es/bitstream/10261/11354/1/Informe2009-Repositorios_0.pdf*.

NISO Framework Working Group (2007) *A Framework of Guidance for Building Good Digital Collections*. Baltimore: National Information Standards Organization. Available from: *http://www.niso.org/publications/rp/framework3.pdf*.

O'Reilly, T. (2005) *What is Web 2.0: Design Patterns and Business Models for the Next Generation of Software*. Available from: *http://oreilly.com/web2/archive/what-is-web-20.html*.

Ottaviani, J. and Hank, C. (2009) 'Libraries should lead the institutional repository initiative and development at their institutions', *Bulletin of the American Society for Information Science and Technology*, 35(4). Available from: *http://www.asis.org/Bulletin/Apr-09/AprMay09_Ottaviani-Hank.pdf*.

Prenafeta, J. (2009) *Contenido de los derechos de autor: Derechos morales y derechos patrimoniales*. Available from: *http://es.safecreative.net/2009/01/15/contenido-de-los-derechos-de-autor-derechos-morales-y-derechos-patrimoniales*.

Read, M. (2008) 'Libraries and repositories', *New Review of Academic Librarianship*, 14: 71–8.

Rodríguez Gairín, J.M. *et al.* (2006) 'Sindicación de contenidos en un portal de revistas: Temaria', *El profesional de la información*, 15(3): 214–21.

Rowlands, I., Nicholas, D. and Huntington, P. (2004) 'Scholarly communication in the digital environment: What do authors want?', *Learned Publishing*, 17(4): 261–73.

Rumsey, S. and O'Steen, B. (2008) 'OAI-ORE, PRESERV2 and digital preservation', *Ariadne*, 57. Available from: *http://www.ariadne.ac.uk/issue57/rumsey-osteen/*.

Scottish Library and Information Council. (2009) *Guide to Using Web 2.0 in Libraries.* Available from: *http://www. slainte.org.uk/files/pdf/web2/Web2GuidelinesFinal.pdf.*

Scovill, L. (1995) *Librarians and Publishers in the Scholarly Information Process: Transition in the Electronic Age.* New York: Association of American Publishers.

Smith, A. (1999) *Why Digitize.* Available from: *http://www. clir.org/pubs/reports/pub80-smith/pub80.html.*

Suber, P. (2007) *Budapest Open Access Initiative: Frequently Asked Questions.* Available from: *http://www.earlham. edu/~peters/fos/boaifaq.htm.*

Swan, A. and Brown, S. (2005) *Open Access Self-archiving: An Author Study – Key Perspectives.* Available from: *http://www.jisc.ac.uk/uploaded_documents/Open% 20Access%20Self%20Archiving-an%20author%20 study.pdf.*

van Eijndhoven, K. and van der Graaf, M. (2007) *Inventory Study into the Present Type and Level of OAI Compliant Digital Repository Activities in the EU.* Available from: *http://www.driver-support.eu/documents/DRIVER%20 Inventory%20study%202007.pdf.*

Willett, P. (2009) 'Mass digitization and its impact on interlending and document supply', *Interlending & Document Supply*, 37(3): 143–8.

Zhang, A.B. and Gourley, D. (2008) *Creating Digital Collections: A Practical Guide.* Oxford: Chandos.

Zuccala, A., Oppenheim, C. and Dhiensa, R. (2008) 'Managing and evaluating digital repositories', *Information Research*, 13(1). Available from: *http://informationr.net/ir/13–1/ paper333.html.*

Index